Presented to

from

on

Little Visits

with

JESUS

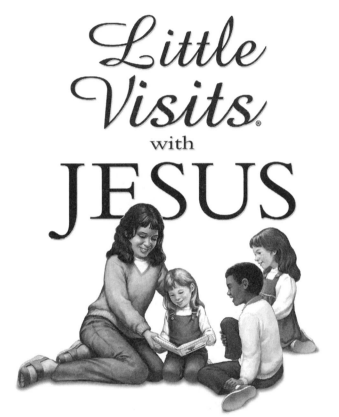

Dr. Mary Manz Simon

Illustrated by Beverly Warren

CONCORDIA PUBLISHING HOUSE · SAINT LOUIS

★

For our grandchildren,
Nate, Luke, and Josh
Psalm 78:4

This edition published 2011
Copyright © 1987, 1990, 1995 Concordia Publishing House
3558 S. Jefferson Avenue, St. Louis, MO 63118-3968
1-800-325-3040 • www.cph.org

Little Visits® is a registered trademark of Concordia Publishing House

Cover illustration © 2011 CPH by John Walker

Scripture quotations are from the Good News Translation in Today's English Version-
Second Edition Copyright © 1992 by American Bible Society. Used by permission.

Manufactured in the United States of America
Chelsea, MI / 055770 / 300435

1 2 3 4 5 6 7 8 9 10   20 19 18 17 16 15 14 13 12 11

The Little Visits® Library

Little Visits with God
Little Visits with Jesus
Little Visits for Toddlers
Little Visits at Bedtime

Books by Dr. Mary Manz Simon

HEAR ME READ SERIES LEVEL 1

What Next? ★ Follow That Star
Drip Drop ★ Row the Boat
Jibber Jabber ★ Rumble, Rumble
Hide the Baby ★ Who Will Help?
Toot! Toot! ★ Sit Down
Bing! ★ Come to Jesus
Whoops! ★ Too Tall, Too Small
Send a Baby ★ Hurry, Hurry!
A Silent Night ★ Where Is Jesus?

HEAR ME READ SERIES LEVEL 2

The No-Go King ★ The First Christmas
Hurray for the Lord's Army ★ Through the Roof
The Hide-and-Seek Prince ★ A Walk on the Waves
Daniel and the Tattletales ★ Thank You, Jesus

The Hear-Me-Read Bible
God's Children Pray

Contents

Preface

Our family's children really matter to me. I do everything possible to help them grow and develop. I'm aware of the importance of "bonding" with young children and that such time together has a positive influence on later relationships.

Young children also need a different, yet equally important, bonding time—one with Jesus Christ. In our home, we call it "Jesus time." During this time of the day, we learn together about the Savior who lived, died, and rose for all, even for our three-year-old.

Family devotions are important. The practice says to children that faith is not just for Sunday mornings in church—it is part of daily living.

Because many families have few opportunities during the day when everyone can be together, family devotions also are a joy. "Jesus time" provides a daily opportunity for all of us to grow closer to each other as we grow spiritually closer to our Lord.

In whatever setting you use this book—around the kitchen table, on the edge of a bed, or in an early childhood classroom—I pray it will help you grow in your understanding of and relationship to a child whom you love and a God who loves you both.

I also pray that your young child—God's gift to you—may enjoy a growing relationship with you as a caring person and with the Savior of all, Jesus Christ.

MARY MANZ SIMON

Suggestions for Use

1. While older children can benefit from these devotions, they are intended for use with young children. Use this book once your child is old enough to express feelings and thoughts in even a few words. We began developing these devotions when our son was less than a year old. At the time, he probably didn't benefit from the content, but he did learn that we talk to Jesus every day. That's important for a person of any age.

2. Try to set aside one specific time each day for "Jesus time"—bedtime, before breakfast, after mid-morning snacks, etc. These very brief devotions will fit into almost any schedule.

3. Twenty devotions are provided for each month—approximately five per week. This allows you the freedom to extend a devotion into a second day, to create your own based on an important family event, or to consider Sunday worship at church as that day's "Jesus time." Also, because children mature rapidly at this age, repeating a devotion a month later will bring different responses and invite greater insights.

4. When possible, personalize the devotions as you use them. For example, substitute the name of your child for the name of the child in the devotion.

5. Whenever a devotion calls for responses, use whatever response your child offers to start a conversation, to extend your child's learning, or to clarify a meaning or feeling.

6. Scripture readings are listed at the top of the page along with a pertinent excerpt. Whenever possible, read the selection from the Bible that belongs to your child. Or, as this book does, you might use Today's English Version (the *Good News Bible*) because of its simple language.

7. The devotions assume active adult participation along with your child's. When there are questions, talk about your responses as well as your child's. When an activity is suggested, participate with your child. In doing so, you, too, will grow in faith.

Little Visits® with Jesus

His love is eternal.
Psalm 118:29

Happy New Year

Do you have a new calendar at your house? Today we start a new year. Sometimes starting new things can be scary. Were you ever scared when you started something new? Were you ever excited when you started something new?

Even though we are starting a new year, we will eat the same kinds of food we ate last year. What would you like to eat this year?

You will probably play with the same toys. What would you like to play with this year?

You are still loved by Jesus. He will love you this year just as much as last year. Last year, this new year, and even next year, Jesus will love you.

Dear Jesus,

It's a new year, and _____.
Some people get excited about New Year's Day, Jesus.
I'm just glad You'll always be my Friend. Amen.

I will never forget you.
Isaiah 49:15

It's No Joke

Bethany and her friends were telling jokes. She asked, "What's green with red spots?"

"A polka-dot alligator?" guessed one friend.

"A Christmas tree with red ornaments?" guessed another.

What do you think is green with red spots?

"Well, Bethany, what is green with red spots?" her friends asked impatiently.

Bethany frowned. "I can't remember!" she said. Everyone smiled.

We forget lots of things, but one thing we should always remember: Jesus is our Savior. That's no joke; that's for real—and it can make us smile. (Bethany just remembered the answer to the joke: What's green with red spots? A pickle with chicken pox.)

Dear Jesus,
Thanks for giving me so many things to smile about. Amen.

Obey your parents ...
Colossians 3:20

Daddies and Fathers

"When I'm a daddy, can I yell?" Joshua James asked his father.

"Oh, Josh, is that all I do as a father?" Dad asked.

"Well, you sure yell loud when you're mad," Joshua James answered.

"Why do you think I yell?" Dad asked.

" 'Cause sometimes I don't do what you tell me. If you yell, that means I really need to obey," Joshua James said.

"That's right. Now it's my turn to ask a question. Do you like it when I yell?" Dad asked.

"No!" replied Joshua James.

"Then let's try something," said his dad. "I'll try not to yell when I'm angry, and you can try to obey. Then we'll both feel better."

Dear Jesus,

Help me obey my parents. I usually know what's right. Help me do what's right. Amen.

Let us go to the Lord's house.
Psalm 122:1

Church Time Again?

Who works at your church? Listen to this story and see if you're surprised who works at Lioba's church.

"Hurry up, Lioba," Mother said. "We don't want to be late for church."

"Why do we have to go again?" Lioba asked. "We went at least a million times at Christmas. I'm tired of church."

"I need to go," Mother answered. "That's my time without the phone ringing or things to do. I can pray and work with God."

"That's silly," said Lioba. "How do you work with God when all you do is sit and be quiet?"

"I think about what's happening," said Mother. "I work inside my head. I think about what the words mean that I say and hear."

"Oh," said Lioba. "I never thought about my head working at church. I'll try that today."

What do you think about when you go to church?

Dear Jesus,

I know that going to church can mean different things to different people. Some people like to hear the pretty music. Some like the nice windows. I like _____ _____ in church. Amen.

Some men who studied the stars came from the East to Jerusalem.
Matthew 2:1–2

Day Number Eleven

Joel was excited about today. It was the eleventh day after Christmas. Epiphany, or "Old Christmas Day" as Nana called it, was tomorrow.

Some Wise Men had visited baby Jesus on the first Epiphany. To remember that time and the rich gifts brought to Jesus, Joel's family decorated the manger set at their house to look like a king was expected.

Nana gave Joel and Tammy a roll of foil paper. They got out a little bag they had stuffed with bits of fabric, paper, and other tidbits.

Tammy started to make a shining thing with points. She folded the foil carefully. She was going to tape this foil item to a stick behind the créche. It would look like it was in the sky. What do you think she was making?

Joel worked with different bits of fabric. What do you think he was making?

Dear Jesus,

Thank You that Christmas keeps going on and on … just like Your love for me. Amen.

And so they left.
Matthew 2:9–11

Happy "Old Christmas"

Tammy quickly hopped out of bed. Then she hurried to get dressed. Today was the twelfth day after Christmas, or "Old Christmas" as Nana called it. This would be a busy day.

Tammy and her brother, Joel, helped Nana take down the holiday decorations. The stack of Christmas boxes was taller than Tammy. Finally everything was put away except the tree and manger.

After supper, everyone gathered around the manger. They sang Christmas carols one last time. Then everyone got to open one last gift. What fun to have another Christmas present!

Tammy and Joel reached for their coats as Nana dragged the Christmas tree out the front door. They were going to watch the cutting of the Christmas tree. Chop, chop, chop. Logs and bigger twigs were stacked in a special place next to the wood pile. Tammy and Joel knew they would burn logs from this Christmas tree in the fireplace next Christmas.

When the last part of the tree had been chopped up, Tammy knew Christmas was really over. Tammy felt happy when she went to bed that night, but she wondered how other children celebrate Old Christmas Day. What did you do on this twelfth day after Christmas?

Prayer suggestion: Talk to Jesus about your day.

I will remember Your great deeds.
Psalm 77:11–12

Special Time

Bedtime was Chad's favorite time of day. He had listened to a story, brushed his teeth, and said prayers with his mom.

Chad heard his mother go down the stairs. The hall light clicked on just as it did every night. Now was his special time. This was Chad's "Jesus time."

Chad lay in bed and remembered as many things as possible that had happened during the day. Then he talked quietly to Jesus. It was fun having a Friend no one could see but who still listened. Chad loved talking to Jesus all by himself.

When is your special time alone with Jesus?

Prayer suggestion: Spend your "Jesus time" telling Him about your day.

Friends

Shelly and Dana were best friends. They liked to do lots of things together. They jumped rope together. They went to the park together. They even went to school together.

But on Sundays, they didn't go to church together. On Sunday mornings, Shelly could see Dana peeking through the window as Shelly's family left for church.

One day, Shelly talked to her pastor about Dana. Shelly said, "Pastor Hank, I want my friend to come to church. What should I do?"

What do you think Pastor Hank suggested?

Dear Jesus,

Help me think of lots of different ways I can invite people to my church. I know I can mail invitations. My family can even offer to bring people to church when we go. Help me remember that going to church is even more fun when I go with a friend. Amen.

He went out, carrying His cross.
John 19:17–18

A Cross Search

"That must be a Bible," said Alex, pointing to a book on the table.

"How do you know?" Grandmother asked.

"It has a cross on it," Alex answered. "That's what the Bible is all about: Jesus died on a cross."

"And look what I always wear," Grandmother said. "Your grandpa gave me this necklace with a cross many years ago. I've never taken it off."

"Never?" Alex asked.

"Never," she answered. "Come now, let's see how many more crosses we can find."

Alex and his grandmother walked around the house. They found one cross with two circles on it in his parents' room.

"That was on your parents' wedding cake," Grandmother said.

Alex even found a cross outside the front door. "That shows everybody that we love Jesus," said Alex.

Alex and his grandmother found four crosses at their house. How many crosses can you find at your house? Ask someone to help you look.

Dear Jesus,
Help me always remember what the cross means. Amen.

Our Lord, Your greatness is
seen in all the world!
Psalm 8:1, 3–4

Thanks, God!

Why are train tunnels round?

Do birds cry?

How do stars shine?

Can you answer any of these questions? I can't without some help from good books.

I didn't make up those questions. A little boy asked them. What a good mind God gave that little boy. And what a wonderful mind God has given you.

You can ask questions. You can answer questions. You can look at pictures, read books, and go places that will help you learn many things about our world.

Today when you talk to Jesus, thank Him for a good mind. God has blessed *you* with the wonderful ability to think.

Dear Jesus,

Thank You for letting me think. I like to think about some of my favorite things, like _____ . Amen.

Why are you so frightened?
Matthew 8:23–27

Nightmares

Drew sat up in bed. He was shaking. He was scared. "Don't make it come true; don't make it come true," Drew kept crying.

Drew had dreamed a bad nightmare. He was worried that what he had dreamed about would really happen.

Have you ever had a bad dream? Share it with the person who is reading to you. Jesus also wants to hear about things that bother you. You can always talk to Him, even if nobody else is around. He will hear you. Jesus will always listen.

Dear Jesus,

Thank You for knowing how scared I sometimes get. Please help me remember I can always talk to You. Amen.

Some friends are more loyal than brothers.
Proverbs 18:24

Where's the Piece?

Outside Paula's house, the weather was blustery. The wind blew cold air all around the house. Inside, Paula and Lana were warm and cozy.

It was a perfect time to work a puzzle. Lana did the bottom half of the puzzle. Paula worked at the top. Carefully they fit together the two halves.

But one piece was missing! They looked and looked. There was the piece—under the box lid. At last the puzzle was done. How neat that felt! And what fun the girls had.

How do you spend wintry days?

Dear Jesus,

Thank You for some of the things I forget to mention all the time: friends to play with; toys to use; and in winter, a place to keep warm. Amen.

God will wipe away every tear from their eyes.
Revelation 7:16–17

A Corner of Heaven

Angela started her prayers with this one night:

Dear God, please take care of Mr. Gain in heaven.

Mr. Gain was a friend of Angela. He had just died. Angela knew Mr. Gain was with Jesus in heaven, but she still wanted to talk to God about it.

Angela did something else. She drew a picture of Mr. Gain's corner of heaven. In heaven, we will have everything we need, so Angela colored a picture of where she thought Mr. Gain was living with Jesus. In her picture, Mr. Gain had a nice green riding lawn mower and some new tools.

Has someone you know died? Draw a picture of their corner of heaven.

Prayer suggestion: Talk to Jesus about any friends or family members who have died. Tell Him how you feel.

How good it is to give thanks to You, O Lord.
Psalm 92:1

Will the Tooth Fairy Come?

Brittany wiggled and wiggled. She used her tongue to push, too. Finally her loose tooth came out.

Brittany carefully wrapped up the tooth. She put it under the pillow on her bed. Brittany hoped the tooth fairy would come that night and leave her some money.

Somebody watched all this. The peeker was Bobby, Brittany's little brother. He was three years old. Can you guess what Bobby did?

First, Bobby tried to wiggle all his teeth. Nothing happened. Then Bobby thought and thought and thought. Bobby went outside. He found a pinecone. He put the pinecone under his pillow.

Then Bobby told his mother, "Mommy, I'm ready for the pinecone fairy to come tonight and leave me some money." Do you think the pinecone fairy visited Bobby?

Sometimes we want something very much. First, Bobby wanted to have a loose tooth like his older sister. Then Bobby wanted to have a visit from a fairy. What is something you wish for?

Dear Jesus,

I know I can't have everything I want. Please help me remember to say thank you when I get something. Please help me accept times when I can't have what I want. Amen.

Praise His name with dancing.
Psalm 149:1–3

All about *J*

What is this letter? (Point to the letter *J* in the title.)

J begins many words. See if you can answer these riddles. Each answer will start with a *J*.

You spread this on bread: _____.

The name of this month: _____.

A person you learn about at Sunday school:

_____.

Now do something that starts with *J*.

Did you jump? We can jump with joy because Jesus loves us. *J* starts lots of words, like jelly, jam, January, and jump.

J is for Jesus, too. And Jesus is the most important *J* word of all! Jesus died on the cross for us. That's worth jumping for joy at least one more time. Ready, get set, jump!

Dear Jesus,

I just jumped for joy. Just, jumped, and joy are *J* words. You are a *J* word, too. Thank You for loving me. Amen.

I will show you my faith by my actions.
James 2:18

Are You a Showoff?

"Showoff, showoff, you're just a showoff." Have you ever said those words? What is a showoff anyway?

Sometimes being a showoff isn't good. It's not good to brag. But you can show off in some nice ways.

You can show a friend something new. You can show someone you care by doing something nice for him. You can ask a person to come see your church or Sunday school.

You can show someone you love her. Do that right now with the person who's reading this book. What's another way you could show someone you love her?

Dear Jesus,

Thank You for showing how much You love me by forgiving me when I do something wrong. You showed me the greatest love when You died on the cross. You also show Your love by putting people around me who love me. Thank You, Jesus. Amen.

Listen, all of you, to the voice of God.
Job 37:1–5

Our Powerful God

It was a stormy day. Even though it wasn't nighttime, the sky was dark, covered with big clouds. When a flash of lightning brightened the sky, Jamal said, "I think I know how God makes lightning. He uses a big flashlight."

A little later, the thunder stopped. The lightning didn't flash anymore, and Jamal said, "It stopped raining. God turned off the faucets."

Jamal didn't really understand what caused the rain to fall and what made the lightning happen. (Ask an adult to help you find the answers.) But he was right about one thing: God is in charge. God is powerful. He made nature.

Now, let's try something. Clap your hands. That's what happens when it thunders. Cold air bumps into warm air and makes a noise. That's just like what happens when one hand touches your other hand in a "clap." That's how God makes thunder.

Everything that happens in our weather isn't as easy to understand, but one thing is sure: God is in charge.

Dear God,
     Thank You for protecting me. Amen.

See how much the Father has loved us!
1 John 3:1

Happy Birthday to Me

"Will I still be a kid after my birthday today?" Matthew asked his aunt.

"Yes," she smiled. "You still have years of being a kid."

"Will I still have blond hair after my birthday?" Matthew asked.

"Why, Matthew, of course," she replied. "You know you've been blond since about your first birthday."

"Will I still ..." Matthew started to ask, but his aunt interrupted.

"Oh, Matthew, don't ask more questions. I'll still love you, too, after your birthday. Now go ahead and play," his aunt said.

Someone else will still love Matthew, too. Can you think who that might be?

Dear Jesus,
Thank You for always loving me. Amen.

You give them food when they need it.
Psalm 145:15–16

What's Your Favorite Snack?

This is a true story.

"I'm hungry, Mommy," said Robert.

"Have a piece of cheese," said Mommy.

"No, I'm hungry for something else," said Robert.

"There's some blueberry yogurt in the refrigerator. Help yourself," said Mommy.

"No," said Robert.

"How about a carrot?" Mommy offered. "I'll even peel it for you."

"No, no, no. That's all food that's good for you. I don't want it," said Robert.

Did anything like this ever happen to you?

God gives us all kinds of food. He wants us to keep our bodies healthy. How do you thank God for your food? Show God now.

Prayer suggestion: Use Psalm 145:15–16 as your table prayer.

God sent His own Son.
Galatians 4:4–5

Remember Christmas?

Caitlyn couldn't believe what she saw. As she and her mom were driving past church, Caitlyn saw that the Christmas stable was still out in front. It was empty. Mary, Joseph, baby Jesus, and all the other figures were gone.

"Mommy, look," Caitlyn said as she pointed out the window. "Why didn't they put away the stable?"

"I heard some people talking about that last week," Mother replied, smiling. "All the manger figures that sat on top of the ground were put away after Epiphany. But the stable posts that are sunk into the ground are frozen in place. The stable might be out there until spring."

"That's all right," said Caitlyn. "It helps me remember Christmas."

What do you remember about Christmas?

Dear Jesus,
I remember when it was Your birthday. Thank You for Christmas. Amen.

I wait eagerly for the Lord's help.
Psalm 130:1–2, 5

A Band-Aid Day

Vincent had a tough morning. He woke up late. Then he put on one brown sock and one blue sock and had to do it over. The oatmeal was cold by the time he got to the breakfast table. The weather was cold, and Vincent had to wear the purple plaid scarf he didn't like. Then he slipped on some ice on the sidewalk. Vincent walked carefully back inside to get a Band-Aid.

Poor Vincent. Have you ever had a day like that?

That evening, when Vincent said his prayers, his mom reminded him he had to thank God for something. Vincent thought a long time.

Finally he had something to say. This was his prayer:

Dear Jesus, thank You for Band-Aids, for medicine, for clean handkerchiefs, and for not having the snow melt yet. Amen.

Have you ever had
a Band-Aid day?

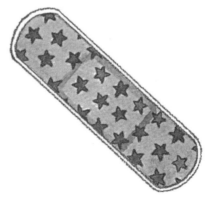

Prayer suggestion: Talk to Jesus about your Band-Aid day.

*Everyone who believes in Him [will] not
die but have eternal life.*
John 3:16

Where?

Ross had a favorite winter activity. He loved to tromp around in the snow. Ross was outside making footprints when he heard a siren.

The ambulance sped by Ross, then turned at the next corner. Soon the ambulance came back. The siren was blaring, and the tires skidded on the snow-packed street.

Later, Ross learned more about the ambulance. Mr. Basian, Ross's neighbor, had a heart attack while shoveling snow. Mr. Basian died, even though many people tried to help him.

After that winter day, Ross asked many questions about people dying. He asked his mom if people could die shopping in a store. He asked his sister if someone could die riding a tractor. He asked his teacher if you could die in an ambulance.

People can die anywhere. But Ross's mom told him the best thing: If you love Jesus, it doesn't matter where you die because you will go to heaven to live with Jesus.

Prayer suggestion: If you know someone who has died, talk to Jesus about that person.

If you refuse good advice,
you are asking for trouble.
Proverbs 13:13

An Easy Way?

Kareem looked outside. The world was white. It had snowed overnight. He couldn't wait to go out and play.

"Now be careful," warned Mother. "There might be ice on the sidewalk."

"Okay, okay—just hurry. I want to get going," Kareem said impatiently as his mother tied his scarf.

Minutes later, Kareem came into the house crying.

"I fell on the ice," he sobbed.

"Well, why did you step on the ice?" Mother asked.

"The ice was in my way," Kareem answered.

Kareem's trouble was right in the middle of the sidewalk. He could have taken a couple more seconds to walk on the other part of the sidewalk, but Kareem tromped right into trouble.

Sometimes it takes more time or trying a bit harder to keep out of trouble. What do you think Kareem will do the next time he sees ice in the middle of the sidewalk? What would you do?

Dear Jesus,

Listening isn't always easy, and I don't always follow good advice. Help me be a better listener. Amen.

His love is made perfect in us.
1 John 4:12

Loving All Your Life

Rosa always liked this time after church. She thought it was fun to shake the pastor's hand when he was still all dressed up in "church clothes."

"I'm going to be a pastor when I grow up," Rosa's brother told Pastor Nickel today. "I want to be just like you."

Rosa listened as her brother and the pastor talked a bit. Pastor Nickel was all smiles. Rosa wondered: What could *I* say to make Pastor Nickel smile and be happy?

"Good morning, Rosa," said Pastor Nickel. "How are you today?"

"I'm going to love Jesus when I grow up," Rosa said.

"I'm going to be a grocery checker at the store when I grow up, but I can still love Jesus."

"Why yes, Rosa," said Pastor Nickel with a big smile. "Even if you choose to drive a big fire truck when you grow up, you can still love Jesus."

Act out a job you might have when you grow up. When you do that job, you can show God's love, too.

Dear Jesus,

I can do lots of things when I grow up. I love You now. I can still love You when I'm much, much older, too. Amen.

Your Word is a lamp to guide me.
Psalm 119:105

A Stormy Night

The rain was beating against the windows. Lightning flashed. Thunder seemed to shake the whole building. Shelly was very afraid.

"Daddy, I don't like the storm," Shelly said. "I'm ..."

Just then the lights blinked out. The electricity had gone off.

"Well, it's a good thing it's bedtime. We wouldn't need lights much longer anyway," Daddy said cheerfully. "Help me look for a flashlight."

Shelly followed her dad to the closet. Then they looked in a drawer. There it was.

"Okay, Shelly, let's go find your pajamas," Daddy said. Her dad held the flashlight so Shelly could brush her teeth. As she brushed, the light grew dimmer. What do you think happened next?

Every night, Shelly listened to a different Bible story. But tonight her daddy couldn't read to her. "We can't read a story without a flashlight," Shelly's dad said. "Tonight why don't *you* tell *me* a story."

Shelly thought of one of her favorite stories. Then she started telling about Daniel in the lions' den.

Pretend you are Shelly now. The lights are off. You don't have a flashlight that works. Tell your favorite Bible story.

Dear Jesus,
Thank You for the brightness of lights. Thank You for the coziness of the dark. Thank You for the Bible. Amen.

*There is nothing ... that will ever be able to
separate us from the love of God.*
Romans 8:38–39

Surprises

There are lots of surprises at Kevin's house.

Kevin's mom is surprised at all the things he leaves on the floor. Is someone at your house surprised at what you forget to put away?

Kevin's dad was surprised when he saw his pictures. He thought the photos would be great—they weren't!

Grandma was very surprised how fast the spinach cooked for supper.

Kevin is often surprised that Jesus still loves him. Sometimes Kevin forgets to be kind—but Jesus still loves him. Sometimes Kevin forgets to say loving words—but Jesus still loves him. Sometimes Kevin doesn't even say "I'm sorry" when he does something wrong—but Jesus still loves him.

Jesus forgives Kevin and continues to love him. Jesus forgives each of us and continues to love us, too. Are you surprised?

Dear Jesus,

Thank You for surprising me with Your love and Your love and Your love. Amen.

All the wild birds are Mine.
Psalm 50:11

Feed the Birds

"Whew, it's cold out there," said Timothy's father. He shook loose snow off his coat. He banged his boots. Little water puddles formed on the boot rack from melting snow.

"Why do you bother to fill the bird feeder when it's so cold?" Timothy asked. "Can't the birds wait till it's warmer?"

"Well, my father used to feed the birds just like I do now," Dad explained. "Your grandpa always used to say that God tells some of the birds to fly to warmer places in winter. Others stay where they are.

"My dad also said God reminded him to take care of the birds just like God took care of him," Dad continued. "That's why I feed the birds even when it's below zero outside."

"Maybe I'll tell my little boy the same story when I grow up," said Timothy. "I'll always remember to feed the birds."

Dear Jesus,

Thank You for taking care of me when the weather is cold. I love You, Jesus. Amen.

*Jesus ... saw a very poor widow
dropping in two little copper coins.*
Luke 21:1–4

Counting Pennies

Midori loved Saturday nights. That was when she got to count the week's pennies.

There was a little cup on the kitchen counter. If Daddy had any pennies in his pockets, he put them in the cup. On Saturday nights, Midori got to look through her mother's purse for pennies. Midori put any that she found into the penny cup. Sometimes Midori even added her own pennies. She had found a couple on the ground.

On some Saturdays, the penny cup was almost empty. Other weeks, the penny cup was really heavy. How many pennies do you think Midori will count this Saturday night?

There's a special reason Midori counts pennies at the end of the week. After she counts them, she puts them in her purse. Then she takes them to church on Sunday morning.

Midori loves Sunday mornings, too. She feels so good putting the coins into the special bank at church. Midori thinks of the children who might hear about Jesus just because of her penny cup.

Do you have a penny cup in your kitchen?

Dear Jesus,

I am working to share my toys. Help me also share my money. Amen.

Children, it is your Christian duty
to obey your parents.
Ephesians 6:1–4

Mommy's Hard Day

"Good night, Megan," Mommy said as she clicked out the light.

Megan's mom waited to hear, "Good night, Mommy, I love you," but Megan didn't say anything. Mother just sighed. It had been a long, hard day. Megan must still be upset she had to go to bed early, Mother thought.

Megan's mother went to the kitchen. Her feet hurt. The sink was full of dirty dishes. She still had to pack lunches for school and work tomorrow. But Mother just sat and thought.

She didn't like it when Megan disobeyed. Megan knew the rules, but today she just didn't pay much attention. Mother prayed to Jesus.

> *Dear Lord, help me be a good parent.*
> *Give me patience. Help Megan be an obedient*
> *child. Help Megan show me love. Amen.*

How do you show love to your parents?

Prayer suggestion: Talk to Jesus about loving and obeying your parents.

*Since you were a child,
you have known the Holy Scriptures.*
2 Timothy 3:15–17

A Winter Vacation

What fun! Kirk and his dad were going on a winter vacation. It was only for one night. It was only to a hotel in the next town. But it was still exciting!

Kirk opened his backpack. First he put in something he would need tonight. What do you think he packed?

Then he added something he'd put in his mouth, but he wouldn't eat. What could that be?

Next he added a few toys. What toys would you pack for a trip?

Now Kirk was ready. "Here I am, Dad," Kirk said. His dad was still packing. Kirk asked, "Why are you taking a Bible? We'll be back in time for church."

"That's one of the things I do every day, Kirk," said Dad. "Long after you're asleep, I read the Bible. But tonight you can sit up with me. I'll read, and then we can talk about what I read from the Bible."

Who reads the Bible at your house?

Dear Jesus,
Help me make Your teachings part of my life every day.
Amen.

Love comes from God.
1 John 4:7

It's Coming!

Valentine's Day is almost here! Let's play a word game today. Finish the sentences with whatever you think of first.

A valentine usually says, _____.

Getting a valentine makes me _____.

I hope that _____.

People who send valentines _____.

I know who loves me every day of the year:

_____.

Happy Valentine's Day to you!

Dear Jesus,
    Thank You for loving me. Amen.

47

We ... have life through Him.
1 John 4:9–10

Introducing Me!

If a new child moves into your neighborhood, how do you introduce yourself? When a child comes to school for the first time, what do you say about yourself?

"I'm me" is how some children introduce themselves. You might choose to say your name, where you live, or tell what you like to do. Maybe you would tell someone about your favorite books or toys.

You know all about you. But how would you introduce Jesus to a friend?

Dear Jesus,
Sometimes I am afraid to tell my friends about You. Help me remember that You will always love me and help me tell others about You. Amen.

We should love one another.
1 John 4:11

Love Day

This is almost like Christmas, thought Erin. There was mail—lots of it. And some envelopes were even addressed to Erin Shannon!

Erin was having wonderful days this month. She loved to send valentines. She also loved to get valentines.

Erin had some favorite cards. She enjoyed those with jokes. She liked to look at valentines that were colored bright pink. It was especially fun to open cards she knew were made by her friends.

At bedtime, this was Erin's prayer:

> *Dear Jesus, thank You for giving me so many people to love me. I'm glad to have valentines to send to special people, too. Thanks, too, Jesus, for loving me all year round, not just on Valentine's Day. Good night, Jesus.*

Prayer suggestion: Use Erin's prayer as your own.

We have heard of your faith in Christ Jesus.
Colossians 1:1–4

St. Valentine's Day

Deanna was puzzled. She had been waiting and waiting for Valentine's Day. But her teacher said it was going to be *Saint* Valentine's Day.

"Mommy, what's a saint?" Deanna asked when she got home.

"Saints are those who believe that Jesus died for them," Mommy answered. "You are a saint because you are a part of God's church."

"So I'm St. Deanna?"

"Yes, I guess you could say that," laughed Mommy.

"Well, then who is St. Valentine?" Deanna asked.

"St. Valentine was a pastor who died many years ago," Mommy replied. "February 14 is the day when he died. People don't know much about him, but we do know that February 14 is the day we think of those who love us and whom we love."

"Well, you can just call it St. Deanna's Day and give me a valentine anyway," said Deanna.

Who are some people you love?

Prayer suggestion: Thank God for the people you love.

I will give you life as your prize of victory.
Revelation 2:10

St. Valentine's Day—Again!

Deanna was still puzzled about St. Valentine's Day. She had been thinking about what her mother said.

Deanna remembered that St. Valentine was a pastor a long time ago. February 14 was the day he had died. But she couldn't figure out why a sad day—when he had died—had become a holiday.

"Mommy, why isn't St. Valentine's Day on that pastor's birthday?" asked Deanna. "It doesn't seem right to be so happy remembering somebody's 'dead' day."

Deanna's mom didn't know the answer to that question. She called the library to find the answer. She learned that years ago, friends remembered the day a person died as a happy time. They celebrated that person's *heavenly birthday*, the day they went to live with Jesus.

Do you think that was a good idea?

Dear Jesus,

Some things I just don't understand. Thank You for helping me learn new things. Amen.

Nothing Special?

"There's nothing to do," said Asha.

"Go outside and play. It's a beautiful winter day," said Grandpa.

"I don't have anything new to play with," said Asha.

"The sun is shining. Just walk around and soak up the warmth," Mother suggested.

"I'm bored," said Asha.

"Watch the clouds drift by like you do in summer," said Grandma.

What else could Asha do? What did you do today?

Dear Jesus,

Today is another day. A regular day. A winter day. Help me see the many things I can do to stay happy and busy and to do good. Amen.

She spent all her time doing good.
Acts 9:36–42

Wear Jesus

Juanita dashed into the house. She ran straight to her room. Where was the jewelry box?

Pretend to help Juanita look. Pull open a drawer—no, it's not there. Now look another place. Where will you pretend to look now? It's not there, either.

She found it. Juanita looked through everything in the box. There, at the bottom in a corner under the hair barrettes, she found it—her necklace with a cross.

Juanita put it on and ran to show her aunt. "Look, Aunt Mary. Now everybody will know Jesus loves me," Juanita said proudly.

"Oh, Juanita," her aunt laughed. "You don't have to wear a cross for people to know you're a Christian. Everybody can tell you love Jesus just by watching you."

Juanita looked puzzled.

"When you show kindness, you are acting like Jesus wants you to," said Aunt Mary. "Remember that day we helped someone across the street? We were showing Christian love."

"Oh, I get it," Juanita said. "When we took valentines that said 'Jesus loves you' to the nursing home, it was the same as wearing a cross."

How do you show people you are Jesus' child?

Dear Jesus,

I show people I am Your child by doing some kind things. Maybe I could also show people I am Your child by _____. Amen.

My help will come from the Lord.
Psalm 121

A Fire

Lauren and her family were away from home on a vacation. They were having a wonderful time at the beach.

Then the phone rang in the hotel room. A friend from home called to say that Lauren's house had burned down. Lauren and her family got on an airplane and flew home.

They learned a terrible explosion had started fires everywhere in the house. Fire fighters told them that if people had been in the house, they would have died or been terribly hurt.

Lauren didn't have any toys to play with. Her clothes that hadn't burned smelled like smoke.

That night, when Lauren went to bed at a friend's house, her mother thanked God. She was very grateful everyone was safe.

This is a true story. Lauren is a friend of mine. The day after the fire, I thanked God for protecting my friends.

Prayer suggestion: Thank God for a time when He protected you or someone you know from danger.

Everyone who asks will receive.
Luke 11:9–10

Have a Problem?

Some children were talking about problems. Let's listen.

"If you don't want to go to swimming lessons and your parent says you have to, that's a problem," said Jordan.

"If your dad orders a hamburger instead of a cheeseburger, that's a problem," said Devon.

Pretend you are sitting on a chair that is too small. What happens? If you fell off, that's a problem! Pretend you can't get your seatbelt fastened in the car. What will you do?

There are different ways to solve problems. Sometimes it helps to talk to people. You can think about things all by yourself. You can talk to Jesus about problems, too. He will always listen to how you feel.

Dear Jesus,
    Sometimes I have problems. I can ask these people for help: _____. I know I can also talk to You about my problems, and You'll listen. Amen.

*It was while we were still sinners
that Christ died for us!*
Romans 5:6–8

A February Surprise

Put your hands over your eyes—no fair peeking. Take your hands away and say, "Surprise! Surprise!" Was that fun?

Surprise! Surprise! That's what the last day of February says to us. In some years, February has 28 days; in other years, February has 29 days.

Look at a calendar in your house. How many days does February have this year? Surprise!

Dear Jesus,

Thank You for always surprising me at the end of February. I'm not surprised, though, that You love me. I know I'm Your child. If I could surprise You with something extra special, I would _____.
Amen.

The Lord does not let us forget
His wonderful actions.
Psalm 111:4

A Late Valentine

Brian loved to get the mail. It was always exciting to open up the mailbox and reach inside. Today there was a letter for him! That was especially fun.

He opened the envelope. Someone had sent him a valentine.

"Mommy, look what I got!" Brian said. "Did somebody miss Valentine's Day?"

His mother glanced at the card with the big red heart. It was definitely a valentine. She read the note inside.

"It's from Uncle Art," Mother explained. "He was in the hospital last month and didn't get to mail this on time. How nice he remembered you!"

Brian sat down to write a thank-you card and a get-well card to Uncle Art. What do you think Brian said to his uncle?

Dear Jesus,

Thank You for giving me people who love me. Thank You for always loving me, too. Amen.

I love you just as the Father loves Me.
John 15:9

Bored?

"I'm bored," Nicole said to no one in particular.

"I'm bored," Nicole told her aunt.

"I'm bored," Nicole told her brother.

Then Nicole was quiet. She had found something to do. What do you think Nicole was doing?

Nicole was thinking of all the people who loved her. Whom do you think she thought about?

Then Nicole smiled to herself. She was thinking about someone very special. She talked to this person every day but had never met Him. Her aunt read stories about this person from the Bible. Nicole learned about this person at Sunday school. The best thing about this person was that He always loved Nicole, no matter what she did. Whom was Nicole smiling about?

Dear Jesus,
Thank You for being You. Amen.

The message about Christ's death on the cross ...
1 Corinthians 1:18

Signs without Words

Stephen walked home slowly. It was such a lovely spring day for looking around!

A construction worker was putting up some flags around Stephen's neighbor's stairs. The worker looked up as Stephen walked by.

"These flags will keep people off the new steps," the worker explained. "The flags say, 'Keep off.' "

"But I don't see any words," Stephen said.

"Even your little friends will know what these flags mean," the worker said. "Why just look around at all the signs without words in your neighborhood."

Stephen did look around. Sawhorses blocked off the next street. The street was being oiled. The sawhorses said, "Keep away."

A cross peeked out from the bare trees. What did the cross tell Stephen?

Stephen decided to act out his own signs without words. First he pretended to tell someone to be quiet. How would you do that? Then he pretended to be a police officer signaling cars to stop. Now try that.

What other signs can you act out without words?

Dear Jesus,

I see signs of Your love all around. You give me people who take care of me and love me. Thank You for the signs of love I see this spring. Amen.

God has forgiven you through Christ.
Ephesians 4:32

What If?

Here is a word game to play. Put on your imagination hat.

What if it snowed chocolate candy?

What if water turned to lemonade?

What if elephants lived in trees?

Can you think of a word riddle? "What if" is a lot of fun to play with friends. But we don't have to play "What if" with Jesus. We never have to ask, "What if Jesus loved me?" We never have to ask, "What if Jesus forgave me?"

We know He loves us. We know He forgives us. That's no fooling!

Dear Jesus,

Thank You for Your love. I love You. Thank You for forgiving me. Help me forgive others. Amen.

I am the Good Shepherd.
John 10:14–16

Pets

Lacey's class at church was talking about animals. The children were taking turns telling about their pets.

"We buy food for my rabbit," Jon said. "Snowy also likes peelings from carrots and pieces of lettuce."

"My guinea pig eats some of that stuff, too," Kayla added.

It was almost Lacey's turn. She didn't know what to say. There weren't any pets at Lacey's house. Her daddy was allergic to dogs and cats. Lacey's sister had some fish one time, but they died. Even the snail died! What would Lacey say?

It was Lacey's turn.

"I don't have a pet," Lacey said. "But I *am* a pet. I am Jesus' little lamb. Jesus takes care of me just like everybody else takes care of their pets!"

What do you think of Lacey's answer?

Dear Jesus,

I like being Your little lamb. I know You take care of me—just like a shepherd takes care of his sheep. That makes me feel safe. Amen.

*Intelligent people are always
eager and ready to learn.*
Proverbs 18:15

Sharing a Dustpan

Uncle Ken was sweeping. Ryan was playing cars. It was a quiet day.

"Where did the dustpan go?" Uncle Ken asked.

"I don't know," said Ryan. He was drawing a road for his cars on a big piece of cardboard.

Uncle Ken walked around looking for the dustpan. It was red. He should have been able to see it, but he could not find it.

"Ryan, I've got to get this cleaned up before your brother gets home," Uncle Ken said. "Could you help me?"

"Sure," said Ryan. "I just need to draw one more road."

"That's just it," said Uncle Ken. "I'd like to borrow your piece of cardboard. I could use that for a dustpan."

"But I don't want a dirty road for the cars," said Ryan.

Uncle Ken and Ryan waited quietly. They were each thinking. How could they solve the problem?

Then Ryan had an idea. "I don't need the whole cardboard," he said. "You can rip off a piece for a dustpan."

How do you think Ryan felt about his solution? How do you feel after solving a problem?

Dear Jesus,

Thank You for giving me a brain so I can think. I get all kinds of ideas. I think about You, too, as my Savior. Amen.

He listens to my prayers.
Psalm 116:1–2

It's Pretzel Day!

Latasha looked out the window. Another gloomy day. The sun hadn't peeked through the thick clouds for a long time. Latasha's mother, though, bustled around the kitchen happily. "It's pretzel day," she said with a smile.

"Pretzel day?" Latasha asked.

"During this time before Easter, we do different things to remember how important Jesus is to us," Mother explained. "Let me tell you about pretzels and praying."

"Fold your hands, Latasha, as though you were praying," Mother said. Fold your hands like Latasha.

"Now show me another way you can pray," Mother said, and Latasha kneeled. Kneel with Latasha.

"Now cross your arms in front of you," Mother said. Cross your arms like Latasha.

"Long ago, that's how people prayed to God," Mother explained.

"Some people bake rolls with crosses on them to remind them Jesus died on the cross. These are called hot-cross buns," Mother said. "Today we'll make pretzels. That will remind us of the people who prayed to God with their arms crossed, just like a big pretzel."

Dear Jesus,
Thank You for this time before Easter. Amen.

The clouds that bring rain in the springtime—
life is there.
Proverbs 16:15

It's Dropping!

One minute Karen was playing happily outside. Just a moment later, she dashed into the house.

"It's dropping outside, Mommy," she said.

"What's dropping, Karen?" Mommy asked.

"It's raining again," Karen answered. "It's raining such big drops."

"Plants need rain to grow," said Mommy, looking out the window. "Soon the grass will start to turn green, and the flowers will bud."

"Our basement doesn't need rain to grow," said Karen. "I bet my toy shelf will get all wet again."

"Lots of rain is part of spring," Mommy reminded Karen. "There are lots of things you like about spring."

Karen thought a minute. What good things about spring do you think Karen mentioned?

Dear Jesus,

Thank You for the seasons. Every time of year is different. I like some seasons better. I know my favorite season will always come back again next year! Thanks, Jesus. Amen.

I will sing with joy because of You.
Psalm 9:1–2

Don't Climb the Flowers!

Anika was getting ready to play at a friend's house. "Now be polite," Mother said. "Don't climb any trees. You aren't wearing slacks today."

"I won't climb," said Anika. "Rasheeda doesn't have any trees, and the flowers aren't big enough."

Anika and her mother both laughed.

What fun to laugh and play. What fun did you have today?

Prayer suggestion: Share some of your good times with Jesus.

*So the One who came down
is the same One who went up.*
Ephesians 4:10

Zebras and Children

What does a zebra look like? If you said a zebra is an animal with black and white stripes, you're right.

Here's a harder question: What does a baby zebra look like?

If you said a baby zebra is smaller than an adult zebra, you're right. But a baby zebra has *brown* and white stripes! As a zebra grows up, the brown stripes change to black.

We change, too, as we grow. If you started using this book two months ago, you've grown since then.

What is one new thing you've learned recently? Have you visited a new place? Have you met a new person? Have you heard a new Bible story?

There are many ways to grow. However you grow and change, you'll still be you. And that's good!

Dear Jesus,
Thank You for helping me
grow up. Amen.

My word is like the snow and the rain.
Isaiah 55:10–11

Upside Down, Inside Out

Think of all the things you can remember about the story of Noah. Ask someone to read to you from Genesis 6:9–9:17 about Noah and the big flood.

Here's a question: If Noah had been given some umbrellas, how would he have used them?

Would he have turned the umbrellas upside down and used them for little boats?

Would he have stuck the umbrellas into the elephants' trunks to protect the smaller animals as they marched into the ark?

What do you think?

Dear Jesus,

Sometimes I get tired of rain in the spring, but I usually still like umbrellas. Thank You for giving me things to keep me dry. Amen.

You caused abundant rain to fall.
Psalm 68:9

Where Is Spring?

Shane looked glumly out the window. It was still raining! After all the rain already this spring, it was raining again. I'll never get outside to play, Shane thought.

"Where is spring anyway?" Shane asked his dad.

His dad walked to a window. "I'll tell you what, let's go out and find spring. We'll get a couple of umbrellas, put on some boots, and take a walk," he said.

Shane and his dad got ready quickly. It wasn't very cold outside, and a walk in the rain was lots better than sitting in the house.

"First we need to smell spring," Dad said with a smile.

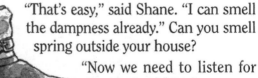

"That's easy," said Shane. "I can smell the dampness already." Can you smell spring outside your house?

"Now we need to listen for spring," said Dad.

"That's easy, too," Shane laughed. "Can't you hear the little raindrops on the umbrellas?" Can you hear a sign of spring outside your window?

Shane's dad asked him to reach out and feel spring. What feels like spring to you? Can you take a spring walk like Shane did?

Dear Jesus,
    Thank You for spring. I especially like _____
_____. Amen.

We are like clay, and You are like the potter.
Isaiah 64:8

Play-Dough Pretending

Pretend you have some clay or play dough on a table in front of you.

Roll it around (just pretend, of course) to get it warm and squishy.

Now shape something that makes you smile. Tell what you made.

Make something that is square. What did you make?

Make something that moves.

Make the face of someone who loves you.

Dear Jesus,
    Thank You for letting me imagine and pretend. Amen.

*Mary remembered all these things
and thought deeply about them.*
Luke 2:19

I Need Christmas

"When is Christmas?" Christy asked her dad.

"It's only March, Christy," Dad answered. "Christmas is nine months away."

"I need Christmas now" Christy said. "I want the pretty lights and my big red stocking. Mostly, I want the feelings."

"The feelings?" Dad asked.

"You know, Daddy—when the air is cuddly and huggy," she replied.

Christy's dad came over and hugged her. "I know what you mean," he said. "The feeling of love that is so strong around Jesus' birthday. But we can have at least some of that feeling any time of year. All we have to do is think about how much Jesus loves us and then love one another."

Dear Jesus,

At Christmas, everybody seems to love everybody else. Help me feel like Christmas every time I remember that You love me. Amen.

Flowers will bloom in the wastelands.
Isaiah 35:1–2

Happy Spring!

"Good morning," said Mother as she came into the bedroom. "We begin a new season today. Happy spring, Alexis!"

Alexis jumped out of bed and ran to the window. The trees still looked bare. The grass was still brown, and there wasn't a flower anywhere.

"It doesn't look like spring," Alexis said. "It doesn't look any different than yesterday."

"Spring is like the earth's birthday," Mother explained. "Do you feel any different the day after your birthday?"

"Well, no," replied Alexis. "I'm sorry things don't look bright and happy like spring should look today. But I can still say, 'Happy Birthday, Earth!' "

Dear Jesus,

Thank You for the promise of newness that we have with spring. Buds promise flowers, and eggs in nests mean baby birds will soon be born. Thank You for this special season. Amen.

[Sent] to be ... Savior.
John 3:17

Looking Ahead

"What are you going to do when you grow up?" Has anyone ever asked you that question?

When you are grown up, you might have a job helping children who are sick. You might cook for people. You might fix streetlights. What else could you do?

When Jesus grew up, He died on the cross for us. He is our Savior. His job was to show how much God loves us and forgives us.

You might do many different things when you grow up. You might be a mother, an aunt, and a computer programmer—all at the same time! When Jesus grew up, He was a preacher and a teacher. But most of all, Jesus is our Savior.

Dear Jesus,

I can call You my Friend. I can call You my Shepherd. Most of all, though, You are my Savior. Amen.

It is I. Don't be afraid!
Mark 6:45–51

Scary Things

Sumiko was watching TV when a flashing dot appeared at the bottom of the screen. Then an announcer broke into the program. The announcer warned of bad weather coming to the area.

Sumiko was scared. She ran straight into the kitchen. "Grandma, Grandma! They said there's a tornado watching. I'm so scared," she said.

"It's probably a tornado watch, Sumiko," Grandma said. "That means there might be a bad windstorm. But come here and let me hug you."

Sumiko settled into her grandma's arms. It wasn't so scary now. Can someone hug you now, too? That feels so good!

Have you ever been afraid of the weather? What are some things that scare you?

Sumiko felt better when her grandma hugged her. Sumiko wasn't as afraid. God gives us people to help care for us. Draw a picture of someone who takes care of you.

Prayer suggestion: Talk to Jesus about what worries you. Then thank Him for giving you people who give you hugs.

A Samaritan ... came upon the man.
Luke 10:30–35

Bumps and Itches

Kara didn't feel good. Her head hurt. Little bumps popped up on her tummy. She itched.

Do you know what was wrong with Kara? She had chicken pox.

Kara didn't sleep well. Kara's grandma got up at night to give her a drink. Kara kept itching. Kara's daddy put on some lotion. Kara was crabby. Kara's sister made her a funny picture.

Do you know what happened? Kara started getting better. The chicken pox didn't itch so much. Her head didn't hurt. Kara wasn't nearly as crabby.

When Kara went to bed, she said this prayer:

Dear God: I hate the chicken pox,
but thank You for taking care of me. Amen.

Can you think of how God took care of Kara?

When we are hurt or sick or scared, God sends people to help us. God took care of Kara by giving her people to help her.

Who has God given to you to help you?

Dear Jesus,

Thank You for people who help when I'm sick, people like Dr. _____. Thank You for someone to help my teeth stay healthy like Dr. _____. Amen.

*Whoever believes in Me will live,
even though he dies.*
John 11:25–27

No Wrinkles in Heaven

Ileana was sitting in one of her favorite places in the whole world: her grandmother's lap. Ileana always felt so safe here, so cozy and so happy.

But today, Ileana was worried. She looked into her grandmother's face. All those wrinkles on Grandma's face and neck must mean that she was getting old, Ileana thought. That worried Ileana.

"Grandma, I've been thinking," Ileana said. "I'm scared you're going to die."

"Does that worry you, Ileana?" Grandma asked.

"Yes, 'cause then I'll miss you, and you won't be here to cuddle me, and we won't sit and talk after you die," Ileana said in one breath.

Grandma smiled and didn't look at all upset.

"You know I will die someday," Grandma said. "And I will miss you. But I'm not worried about dying."

"You aren't?" Ileana asked. She couldn't understand that.

"I'll be with Jesus after I die," Grandma said. "And someday you'll be in heaven with Jesus and me. Maybe I won't even have all these wrinkles on my face."

How do you think Ileana felt after talking with her grandmother?

Prayer suggestion: Talk to Jesus about death and how it makes you feel.

They found the stone rolled away.
Luke 24:1–9

A Present for Easter

"Pablo, why are you so sad today?" Grandpa asked. "Easter's coming."

"Aw, Grandpa. Easter's no fun," said Pablo. "Easter is just eggs, and I hate hard-boiled eggs."

"Well, Pablo, you know you can't have all that sugar in jelly beans and candy," said Grandpa.

"Easter's a no-fun holiday," said Pablo.

Then Grandpa had an idea you can try, too. He and Pablo went outside to look for smooth rocks. They washed them off. Then Pablo painted crosses on the rocks.

Pablo spent the whole afternoon using crayons and markers to make Easter rocks. He couldn't wait to put them into Easter baskets.

Who can help you make Easter rocks?

Dear Jesus,
    Help me remember the real message of Easter. Amen.

The Lord is risen indeed!
Luke 24:28–34

Easter Egg Cartons

"There's nothing to do now," Cody complained.

"Why, Cody, I just spent all morning decorating eggs with you boys," Father said. "How can you say there's nothing to do?"

"Cody's right, Dad," Jason said, "Easter fun is over before Easter even gets here. There's nothing left now."

His father was quiet. Then he said, "Boys, that makes me very sad. We wouldn't even have Easter if Jesus hadn't risen. That's the real meaning of Easter.

"Here, you guys each take an empty egg carton," Dad said. "This afternoon use the egg carton to make something that shows the real meaning of Easter. We'll talk about your Easter egg cartons at supper."

Jason and Cody glumly picked up the cartons.

At supper, each boy proudly brought his Easter egg carton creation. Jason had made a model of the first Easter. He had ripped apart pieces of the egg carton to make the tomb, a garden with trees, and people. He used a tissue to show the tomb where Jesus had been laid.

Ask your parent for an empty egg carton. Use your carton to make what you think Cody made with his Easter egg carton.

Dear Jesus,

I know You are the real reason for Easter. Sometimes, with the Easter eggs and candy, I forget that. Please help me remember Your empty tomb. Amen.

He has been raised from death.
Matthew 28:1–7

Some Easter Fun

Instructions: Play this Eastertime game together.

When I think of Easter, I think of bunnies.
   Can you do something rabbits do?
When I think of Easter, I think of eggs.
   Can you pretend to be a little chick hatching?
When I think of Easter, I think of flowers.
   Can you pretend to grow from a seed into a flower?
When I think of Easter, I think of Jesus.
   Now what can you do?

Dear Jesus,

   I love so much about Easter. I like to hear about the first Easter. That story makes me feel _____ _____. Amen.

*So they entered the tomb, where they
saw a young man ... wearing a white robe.*
Mark 16:1–8

Playing Easter

"Heather, what are you doing?" Mother asked.

"I'm playing Easter," Heather answered. "See? Don't I look like an angel?"

Her mother smiled at Heather's costume. What would you wear to look like an angel?

"I see you found a paper plate for a halo," Mother said. "And that clean sheet does make a nice gown. But Heather, why did you turn the clothes basket upside down?"

"That's the tomb," Heather said happily. "And see, it's empty. Jesus has already jumped out!"

Was Heather right about Easter? Can you act out the story of Easter?

Dear Jesus,
Thank You for the first Easter. Thank You for this Easter. Amen.

Then she ... saw Jesus standing there.
John 20:11–18

Another Easter?

Ashley loved Easter. Unpacking the box of Easter baskets was such fun. And all the pretend grass made a pretty sight inside the baskets. She even got to eat a few candy eggs when she and her mommy fixed little baskets to give to friends. Yes, Easter was a favorite time of year for Ashley.

What do you like about Easter? Can you think of something special you get to eat at Easter? Can you think of what you might wear on Easter?

There was one thing Ashley didn't understand about Easter. Let's listen as she talks with her mommy.

"I thought we had Easter last year, Mommy," Ashley said.

"Of course, we had Easter last year, Ashley," Mommy replied. "We even used the same baskets."

"How can we have Easter again?" Ashley asked. "Does Jesus keep dying and rising every year?"

"No, Jesus died and rose on the first Easter. We just remember that first Easter every year," Mommy answered. "If Jesus hadn't risen, we wouldn't even have an Easter."

Do you have any questions about Easter?

Dear Jesus,
I like the brightness and happy feeling of Easter. Please help me keep that Easter feeling inside me. Amen.

Mary Magdalene went to the tomb.
John 20:1–10

Olden-Day Easters

"Grandpa, what was Easter like in the olden days when you were little?" Jenna asked.

"Well, Jenna," Grandpa said, "we colored eggs in a different way. We did it like my parents did in England when they were little.

"First, I carefully took a raw egg," he explained. "Then I wrapped brown onion skin around the egg and an old rag around that.

"My mother always helped tie a string around the cloth," Grandpa added. "Then the egg was boiled for about 20 minutes.

"When we unwrapped the hard-boiled egg, it was a shade of yellow or brown," Grandpa said.

"Wow, Grandpa! That really is different," Jenna said.

"To make pink eggs, we used rose petals," Grandpa said.

"But let me tell you," Grandpa added, "there's one thing that was the same then for me as it is for you this Easter." What is Grandpa thinking about?

Dear Jesus,

Some things are very different now from years ago. But I know that people went to church a long time ago, just as I go to church now. And they dressed up in their best clothes on Easter Sunday, too. But the most important thing that's the same is You. You are the reason for Easter. Amen.

He is not here; He has been raised.
Luke 24:1–9

No Easter Bunny?

Manuel had lots of fun playing with his friend Claire. But now Manuel was running home. And he was crying.

Manuel raced into the house. "Mommy, Mommy," he called.

"Oh, Mommy," Manuel came up to his mother, "Claire says there's no Easter bunny. If there's no Easter bunny, how can we have Easter?"

Manuel laid his head on his mother's lap and cried. When he calmed down, she talked to him quietly.

"Manuel, your little friend is right about one thing," Mother said. "We don't need a bunny to have Easter. We don't

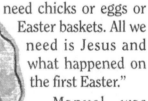

need chicks or eggs or Easter baskets. All we need is Jesus and what happened on the first Easter."

Manuel was quiet. He thought about what his mother said.

You can read in Luke 24:1–9 about the first Easter.

Dear Jesus,
Easter means lots of things. Easter means eggs. Easter means springtime. Easter means _____.
Most of all, Easter means You are alive as my Savior. Amen.

*So He took some soil ... and formed all
the animals and all the birds.*
Genesis 2:19

Animal Riddles

Here are some riddles. Every answer is the name of an animal. See if you can guess the animals.

This animal has a long neck. It has spots. It has very long legs and lives in Africa. Sometimes you see this animal in the zoo. What is it?

This animal barks—but it's not a dog. This animal eats fish—but it's not a whale. This animal sometimes claps its flippers in a zoo show. What is it?

This animal looks like a pig with a hard shell. It has a long tail. It lives in the southern part of the United States, especially in Florida and Texas. What is it?

God made all the animals. He made giraffes, seals, and armadillos. Did you guess them all? God gives us cats to pet and dogs to walk.

What animals do you like best?

Dear Jesus,
Thank You for animals that bark like _____.
Thank You for animals that wag their tails like _____. Thank You for animals that wiggle like _____. Amen.

God will put His angels in charge of you.
Psalm 91:11–12

Afraid of the Dark

"I get afraid at night," Yoshi said. "I think the big bad wolf will climb through the window."

"I always think there is a robber with a gun," said Yasuko. "I stay awake all night."

"I get scared, too," said Rosanne.

"Do your eyes stay open all night, Rosanne?" Yoshi asked.

"Oh, no," said Rosanne. "Mommy told me it's okay to be scared sometimes. That's when I talk to Jesus. Sometimes I sing songs, too," said Rosanne. Sing with her.

> *Jesus loves me, this I know,*
> > *For the Bible tells me so.*
>
> *Little ones to Him belong;*
> > *They are weak, but He is strong.*
>
> *Yes, Jesus loves me, yes, Jesus loves me.*
> > *Yes, Jesus loves me, the Bible tells me so.*

Lots of children are afraid at night. Some children get scared when they walk into a dark room. Maybe even Jesus was afraid when He was a little boy.

Jesus is ready to help you at night. You can sing to Him. You can talk to Him. He even sends someone to watch you at night. Who do you think that is? The answer is in Psalm 91:11–12.

Dear Jesus,

I know Your angels watch over me. Thank You, Jesus. Amen.

Christ died for our sins ...
He was raised to life three days later.
1 Corinthians 15:3–7

Hooray! Hooray!

Instructions: Act out this poem together.

I want to clap my hands. I want to give a cheer.
> Hooray! Hooray! Easter is here.

I want to turn around. I want to stamp my feet.
> Hooray! Hooray! Easter is neat.

I want to tap my head. I'll wiggle an ear.
> Hooray! Hooray! Easter is here.

I want to tap my elbow. I will reach to heaven.
> Hooray! Hooray! Jesus is risen.

My body will shout. I'll tell everyone.
> Hooray! Hooray! Jesus is God's Son.

I'll hold my waist.
> Then I'll touch my nose.
> Hooray! Hooray!
> Jesus Christ rose.

I'll jump on the floor, then sit
right down.
> Hooray! Hooray!
> Jesus wears a crown.

Dear Jesus,
> Thank You for Easter. Amen.

Once there was a man who went out to sow grain.
Mark 4:3–8

Planting Time

"What a great day for planting," Daddy said at breakfast. "I can't wait to spread that grass seed."

"Do you have to plant grass?" Daria asked. "I thought it just grew."

Everyone at the breakfast table laughed. Everybody laughed—except Daddy.

"Let's look," he said. He and Daria walked over to the window. The whole area around their new house was a sea of mud. Mud, mud, mud.

"Won't grass just grow, Daddy?" Daria asked again.

"It won't grow unless we plant it," he answered. "So let's go outside and start it growing."

Daria tried to think of other plants that grew from seeds. Look outside your window. How many things do you see that grew from seeds?

Dear Jesus,

Thank You for seeds that grow, like _____ _____; for seeds I eat, like _____ _____; for seeds that look pretty, like _____. Amen.

I love you.
John 15:9

You Can't See It, But ...

There are at least two answers to today's riddle. See if you can guess them.

> You can't see it.
>
> You can't touch it.
>
> You can't taste it.
>
> But it is everywhere.
>
> What is it?

Did you guess air? You couldn't blow up a balloon without air. You couldn't fly your kite without air. But we can't see it, touch it, or taste it. We need air, though, to live.

Maybe you guessed another answer to the riddle. Did you answer "Jesus' love"? We can't see Jesus' love floating through the air; we can't reach out and grab it; we can't taste Jesus' love. But we need it to live a caring, loving life.

Dear Jesus,

I'm glad You love me. I know I can't see You, but I feel Your love when someone is nice to me. That just happened when _____. I'm glad Your love is all around me. Amen.

You are ... members of the family of God.
Ephesians 2:19

Just the Two of Us

Samantha dragged her feet. It had not been a good day at school. What do you think made Samantha sad?

Samantha's class had talked about families. Then everybody made their houses. The children cut a window out for every member of their family. Samantha only got to cut out two windows. How many windows would you cut out for your family?

"Mommy, it's not fair," Samantha complained as she walked in the front door. "Everybody has a bigger family than we have."

Her mother listened as Samantha explained the school project. "Honey, a bigger family doesn't mean a better family," Mother said. Samantha still looked sad.

Her mother thought for a while. She and Samantha had a lot of good times together. They loved each other a whole lot.

"You know, Samantha," Mother said, "you probably belong to the biggest family of all. You and I both belong to God's family, so we have everything we could want.

"We have the two of us when we want to just be alone, and that's nice," Mother continued. "And when we want to feel part of a bigger family, we just have to remember we're part of God's family."

How do you think Samantha feels now? How many windows would you cut out for your family now? Make a paper house like Samantha's for your family.

Dear Jesus,
Thank You for people who love me. Amen.

Look at the birds ... your Father in heaven takes care of them!
Matthew 6:26–27

Why?

Jo Ellyn and Pierre watched a robin make a nest right outside the window. The bird kept coming to the nest with bits of dead grass. One day, the robin flew in with a long, long string. Then the robin brought something that really surprised Jo Ellyn and Pierre. What do you think that was?

Each day, the children looked out the corner of the window into the nest. At first, the nest looked like a big mess. But every day, the nest was looking neater. The robin wiggled into the grass and twigs to make the nest fit just right.

One day, the robin didn't come to the nest. Nor the next day. The bird that had worked many days making a great nest never came back. What do you think happened to the bird?

Jo Ellyn and Pierre were very disappointed. They felt sad, too. The children never found out what happened to their friendly robin.

Have you ever wondered why something happened? Sometimes there aren't any good answers. We don't understand everything that goes on. But God does. He has a plan for everything and everyone. God will take care of us.

Dear Jesus,

Sometimes I don't understand everything. I know You do. I know that You will always take care of me. Amen.

The Lord ... is good to everyone.
Psalm 145:8–9

At the Airport

Julian stood with his dad and looked out the airport terminal windows. He saw all kinds of cars and trucks and wagons rolling around. This was a busy place!

Then Julian heard a motor start up. What kind of motor could it have been?

Julian turned around. Some people in different kinds of uniforms were walking through the terminal. What kind of work do you think those people did?

Julian turned around quickly to look out the window again. A jumbo jet was taking off.

"Dad, how does God make airplanes fly?" Julian asked.

"God doesn't make the airplanes fly, Julian," Dad answered. "But God did give good minds to people, and some of them figured out how to make airplanes fly."

"Will I be that smart some day?" Julian asked.

"Everybody is good at some things," Dad answered.

"Like I can ride a two-wheeler?" Julian asked.

"Yes, Julian," his dad answered. "God has been very good to you."

God is good to all of us in different ways. How has God been good to you?

Dear Jesus,
Thank You for always caring about me. Amen.

Whoever loves is a child of God.
1 John 4:7

Who Is It?

Many people help care for us. God lets different people help us at different times. Answer these riddles with the name of the person who helps you.

I sit in a special chair. The chair goes up and down. Somebody looks in my mouth. Somebody uses a little mirror to count my teeth. Who is this somebody?

I go here to keep well. I visit this person when I am sick, too. Sometimes I get medicine from this person. I usually feel better when I leave this person. Who is this somebody?

I go here to learn about Jesus. I sing songs and have fun. This person is always glad when I come to Sunday school. Who is this somebody?

I go here when my shoes are too tight. I get new shoes here. This person measures my feet. I put my foot up on a chair with a funny little ramp. Who is this somebody?

Dear Jesus,
    Thank You, Jesus, for the people who help me. Amen.

[God] loved us and sent His Son.
1 John 4:9–10

Shopping Time

Let's pretend we're shopping for food. What's the first thing you do? Act it out. Can the person reading this book guess what you do first in the store?

Now pretend to find one of your favorite foods. Can you reach it on the shelf? Is the package heavy or light? Act it out. Can the person guess what you're going to buy. Did your reader guess right?

Now it's time to check out. Where do you get the money?

We can buy many things at the grocery store. We can get all kinds of food. We can buy all sorts of things for the house. We can even buy a lot of things that aren't groceries.

There's one thing we cannot buy at a grocery store—or anywhere else. That's God's love. We don't have to buy God's love. It's free for you. It's free for me. It's free for everyone.

Prayer suggestion: Thank God for His love.

God looked at everything He had made,
and He was very pleased.
Genesis 1:31

Earth Week at Danielle's House

This was a special month at Danielle's house. Every Sunday in April, something different was set in the middle of the kitchen table. Earlier this month, the family had little Easter bunnies and chicks. Last week, her brother put his favorite truck on the table.

But Danielle really liked this week. A globe sat in the middle of the table. While supper was cooking, Danielle and her brother played a game. Danielle would close her eyes and spin the globe. She would open her eyes, tell whether her finger landed on water or land, and her brother would read the name of the place.

Danielle had learned a lot. She learned that the globe looks like our earth. It is round. It spins. It is tilted sideways a bit. And there is more water than land. The blue color on the globe showed that.

But Danielle didn't know the answer to one question. "How did God make the earth, Daddy?" she asked.

"I wasn't there, Danielle," her father said. "But I do know that God did make it. Let's read in the Bible about what happened."

Danielle and her father sat down to read about creation. Ask someone to read Genesis 1:1–31 to you.

Dear God,

Thank You for making green things that grow, like
_____ ; for making yellow things
that smell good, like _____ ;
and for making everything on Your beautiful earth. Amen.

No one has ever seen God.
1 John 4:12

Let's Play!

Let's play a thinking game. Listen to each riddle, then answer the question. There can be many right answers.

This person lives far away. You don't see this person very often. But when this person and you see each other, the first thing you do is hug each other. Who is this person?

This person lives near you. You are always glad to see this person come. When this person isn't here, you wait eagerly for him. Who is this person?

You see this person a lot. This person doesn't live in your house, though. You always have fun with this person. Who is this person?

You love this person, but never hug Him. You talk to this person, and He never interrupts. This person is here and everywhere else, too. Who is this person?

Dear Jesus,

I really do love You. I talk to You, too. I know You love me. Amen.

The Lord has forgiven you.
Colossians 3:12–13

Somebody Knows Your Secret

Ewaldo threw down his piano books. What an awful lesson he'd had!

"How was your piano lesson, Ewaldo?" Mother asked.

"Horrible," Ewaldo answered. "How did Mrs. Ansley know I didn't practice? Did you tell her, Mom?"

"Oh, no," Mother answered. "She could just tell by how well you knew your lesson."

"How?" Ewaldo asked again.

"Just like the dentist knew last week that you hadn't been brushing your teeth," Mother said. "And just like God knows when you sneak candy to eat in bed at night."

"That's awful!" Ewaldo said angrily. "I'm going to my room! And don't come in!" Ewaldo slammed the door.

Ewaldo felt horrible. It was no use. He did lots of bad things, and he guessed that God knew about everything. Ewaldo felt horrible—until he remembered something. Then he said this prayer:

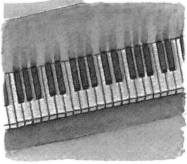

Dear Jesus, I'm sorry I do bad things sometimes. But I just remembered that You forgive me. You still love me. You will always love me. That makes me feel much better. Amen.

Prayer suggestion: Use Ewaldo's prayer as your prayer.

Trust in the Lord now and forever!
Psalm 131:2–3

Why Do I Have to Grow Up?

Timothy decided that he didn't want to grow up. When he was a little boy, it was all right to suck his thumb. But now that he was growing bigger, his father said, "No more thumb sucking!"

Timothy had tried to stop sucking his thumb. Every time he thought about it, he pulled his thumb out of his mouth. His dad said he just didn't think about it enough.

His father said, "You'll have to wear a sock on your hand at night so you can't suck your thumb."

His grandmother said, "Get a drink of water every time you feel like sucking your thumb."

His brother said, "I'll give you a trading card every day you don't suck your thumb."

You tell the end of this story.

Dear Jesus,

It's not easy to grow up. Sometimes my new teeth hurt when they come in. Now that I'm bigger, I have to do more work. Whenever I think about the things I don't like, please help me remember the good things about growing up. Amen.

The Lord has given us eyes to see with.
Proverbs 20:12

Those Wonderful Eyes

Andrea dragged her feet up the steps. She didn't want to go home because as soon as she got home, she would have to get her new eyeglasses.

"Andrea," Mother said as she walked inside, "your new glasses are ready. Have a quick snack and let's go."

Andrea dragged into the kitchen. Mother said, "Honey, I'm sorry you aren't happy about your new glasses."

Andrea looked up. She wasn't smiling.

"Andrea," Mother said. "What did God give you to protect your eyes?"

Andrea felt all around her eyes. What did she feel?

"My eyebrows?" she asked.

"That's right. They help keep dust out of your eyes," Mother explained. "Now gently touch your eyelashes." Touch your eyelashes with Andrea. What happens?

"I can't help blinking," Andrea said.

"That's right," Mother said. "They automatically try to close if something is coming too close to your eyes. Now feel around your eye." Feel around your eye with Andrea.

"There's a bone," Andrea said.

"God made our eyes to be surrounded by things that protect our sight," Mother explained. "I'm just so grateful you have eyes to see. And after today, you'll be able to see even better!"

How do you think Andrea felt now?

Dear Jesus,
I love looking _____. Thank You for my eyes. Amen.

I am putting My bow in the clouds.
Genesis 9:12–17

I Hate Rain!

The day had been beautiful. The new grass was turning green. Some bushes were flowering. And the sun was so warm it even heated up the sand in Mack's sandbox. It had been a beautiful day—until now.

Mack dashed into the house to beat the raindrops. He did not even know it was going to rain. The sky still looked light.

"I hate rain. I hate rain," Mack complained as he rubbed his hair dry with a towel. "Why did it rain, Mommy?"

"It rained so we could have a rainbow, Mack," Mommy answered. "Come here, quickly! Look up."

Mack looked. The colors weren't bright, but he could see a rainbow—a real rainbow. What colors did Mack see in the rainbow? An easy way to remember the colors of the rainbow is to remember *Roy G. Biv*. Each letter of this pretend person's name starts one of the color names: *R*ed, *O*range, *Y*ellow, *G*reen, *B*lue, *I*ndigo, *V*iolet.

"Oh, Mommy," Mack said softly. "It's my first rainbow, my very first rainbow."

They stood and watched out the window until the rainbow was gone.

"Before bed tonight, Mack, let's read the story of the very first rainbow," Mommy said. "Then every time you're unhappy with rain, you can remember your first rainbow and the very first rainbow."

Read about God's first rainbow in Genesis 9:8–17.

Dear Jesus,
Thank You for this color-filled world. Amen.

She gave birth to her first son.
Luke 2:7

Egg Talk

Kenji found something on the ground. It was blue and very thin. It was cracked and small. It had fallen from a nest in a tree. What did he find?

People who study birds are called ornithologists. Birds are hatched. Do you know what *hatch* means?

People don't crack open a shell and hatch. God made a wonderful way for us to be born. Jesus had a mother and was born in the same way as every other person. And God cared for His own Son just as He cares for us.

Ask your parents to tell you about your birth. What did you look like after you were born? Where were you born? Read Luke 2:1–7 and find out about another baby's birth.

Dear Jesus,

I know some animals hatch from eggs, like birds and turtles. But I didn't hatch. I had a real mommy, just as You did when You were born. That makes me feel so special! Amen.

His angel guards those who have
reverence for the Lord.
Psalm 34:7

Voices in the Night

Kirstin rolled over in bed. She was having a hard time getting to sleep on this warm night. The window in her bedroom was open, and Kirstin heard many strange noises. First she heard bugs. Then she heard some birds.

Now she heard voices. Kirstin crept down the stairs. No, it wasn't Daddy talking on the phone.

Kirstin went back to bed. But she still heard voices. Maybe her neighbors were out in the back yard. Kirstin tiptoed to the window. No one was outside.

Kirstin crawled back into bed. Then she heard music, too. So that's it! Kirstin thought. She went to sleep with a smile.

At breakfast the next morning, Kirstin told her father, "Daddy, I heard your angel talking to my angel last night."

Her father looked puzzled.

"I kept hearing voices," Kirstin explained. "Then I heard pretty music, too. That's how I knew it was the angels talking and playing their harps."

Her father put his head back and laughed. "I was listening to a concert on the radio after you went to bed," he said. "But, maybe you did hear angels after all."

What do you think Kirstin really heard?

Dear Jesus,
Thank You for watching over me. Thank You for sending Your angels to protect me, too. Amen.

With them went every kind of animal.
Genesis 7:1–16

A Is for Animal

Gina loved the zoo. Spring at the zoo was the best time of all—there were lots of baby animals.

Gina liked to visit the place where lots of things crawled around. Where in the zoo did Gina go to see these animals?

Gina laughed when she saw other animals swing from their tails. What animals did Gina laugh at?

Gina raced over to see what was barking. What did Gina run to see?

The animals you and Gina see at the zoo are like the ones that took a boat trip a long time ago. You can read the story in Genesis 7:1–16.

What is your favorite animal at the zoo? When you talk to Jesus today, thank Him for that wonderful creature. We know God created all the animals. Aren't you glad of that?

Dear Jesus,

Thank You for animals that wiggle and those that squiggle, for animals with fur and animals that purr, and for all animals. Amen.

*God had not forgotten Noah and all
the animals with him in the boat.*
Genesis 8:1–5

Car Wash Time

Amber loved going through a car wash. Can you act out going through a car wash? Show how the big hose sprays water. Now pretend you are the soap suds. Show how the big, cloth arms wash a car. Now be the giant blow dryer.

"Daddy, if we had a van, how would we get it washed?" Amber asked as the hose sprayed the water.

"We'd need to go to a larger car wash," Daddy said.

"If we had a pickup truck, how would we get it washed?" Amber asked. The soap suds were swishing on the windshield.

"We'd drive the pickup to a truck wash," Daddy answered.

"Daddy, if we had a mobile home, how would we get it washed?" Amber asked. The big cloth arms came over the top of the car, back and forth, back and forth.

"I guess we'd have to pay someone to wash it for us," Daddy said.

Now it was time for the giant blowers to dry their car. Amber had one more question. Can you answer it?

"Daddy, how did Noah keep the ark clean? It wouldn't fit in a car wash," she said.

What would you tell Amber?

Dear Jesus,

Thank You for giving us clean water. We wash our car. We wash our clothes. We wash me. We _____
_____. Help us use water wisely. Amen.

*Clouds that bring rain in the springtime—
life is there.*
Proverbs 16:15

A Spring Walk

Let's take an imaginary walk today. We're going to look for signs of spring. Let's look in the grass first. What signs of spring can you find?

Now let's look up. How many signs of spring can you see? Is one of those spring things moving?

Here's a hard question: Can you find signs of spring on the sidewalk? Look for things that crawl. Can you think of any? Sometimes there are cracks in the sidewalk; are there any signs of spring there?

In spring, God's world wakes up from a winter rest. How do you feel in spring?

Dear Jesus,

Thank You for spring. I especially like _____
_____. Amen.

The Lord God planted a garden in Eden.
Genesis 2:8–9

It's Cleaning Day

Look around where you are sitting. Do you see any dust? Is some hiding behind a chair? under a bed? on the chair bottom?

Jessica's house has a lot of dust. She is helping her father clean. Let's listen as they talk.

"Daddy, why is it dusty already?" Jessica asked. "We did the same cleaning last week."

"Jessica, there's dust almost everywhere," Daddy answered. "Now that the weather is warm, the wind blows dust into the house from outside."

"Let's close the windows," Jessica suggested.

"That won't help much," Daddy said. "Even you make some of the stuff we vacuum up. See? Here's a piece of hair. And last week we found a fingernail. And sometimes your clothes leave bits of thread or lint."

Jessica thought about what her daddy said. She thought of one place where there wasn't any dust. (What place do you think she thought of?)

Jessica thought about the garden God created for the first people on earth. "I'll bet they didn't have cleaning day in the Garden of Eden," Jessica said. Do you think Jessica was right?

Dear Jesus,
Cleaning up isn't always much fun. Help me be cheerful when I work. Amen.

Happy are those who ... die in ... the Lord.
Revelation 14:13

Bigger ... Smaller

"Daddy, I need to tell you something," Neil whispered. "Granny's shrinking."

"That's possible, Neil," Daddy said. "As your great-grandmother has grown older, her body has changed in different ways. It might look like she's shrinking."

"Pretty soon I'll be as tall as she is," Neil said.

"Yes," Daddy smiled. "You are a growing boy."

Neil thought his great-grandmother looked even smaller the next time he visited. But maybe, just maybe, he had grown, too.

"Granny," Neil said. "I'll love you even if you get smaller."

"Neil," said Granny. "I'll love you even if you get bigger."

Neil and Granny both smiled. Neil wondered, though, would he be taller than Granny when they got to heaven? What do you think?

Dear Jesus,

I wonder a lot about heaven. Will I be the same as I am now? Will I have the same friends? I wish I could know more about heaven, but I guess I'll just find out when I get there. Thanks for listening. Amen.

*God made peace through His Son's
death on the cross.*
Colossians 1:20

Shadow Play

"Mommy, can I have a drink of water?" Rachel asked.

"Okay, go downstairs and get one," said Mother. "But then it's bedtime for sure."

"I'm afraid to go down by myself," said Rachel.

"Why?" Mother asked. "I need to tuck Patrick in bed, so I can't go down with you."

"I'm afraid of the shadows," Rachel explained. "They look so scary on the walls."

"Wait a minute," Mother said with a sigh. "I'll go down with you."

A few minutes later, as they stood at the top of the steps, Mother said to Rachel, "Make a cross with your fingers to block out the light as you go down the stairs. What looks like it's going with you?"

"It looks like a cross walking downstairs!" Rachel said.

"You know that Jesus is always watching over you," Mother said. "If you're ever afraid in the dark, just make your fingers in the shape of the cross of Jesus. That will help remind you that you'll never be alone."

Turn on a light in your room. Go very close to the wall. Now make a cross with your fingers like Rachel did. Walk along the wall. You, too, can always take along a reminder of Jesus.

Dear Jesus,

Even though I might be all alone, I don't have to be lonely. I know that You are always with me. Amen.

Lord, You have made so many things!
Psalm 104:10–28

Be Alive!

Instructions: Act out this poem together.

The grass is growing;
It soon will need mowing.
The clouds are moving fast;
How long will the sunshine last?
The wind is starting to blow.
Look! Watch that rabbit go.
I hear the birdies calling.
Now some rain is falling.
God is caring for our earth.
It's spring—the time of new birth.
Chickens hatch. Puppies are born.
Farmers plant wheat, oats, and corn.
Thank You, Jesus, for giving us spring.
Thank You, Jesus, is what I sing.

Prayer suggestion: Sing a song to Jesus as your prayer.

Thumbs Up!

Let's play a game. If the sentence is good, put your thumbs up. If the sentence is not good, put your thumbs down. Let's practice: thumbs up; thumbs down.

I didn't share my toys.

I fussed when I set the table for dinner.

I fussed when I couldn't do what I wanted to do.

I helped rake the grass.

I cleaned up my room.

I brushed my teeth without being told.

I put away my toys.

I am playing this game.

Because you are Jesus' child, playing this game is "thumbs up." That's because you know how Jesus wants you to act. Everybody makes mistakes (that's thumbs-down time), but Jesus always forgives us (and that's thumbs up).

When you're making a decision—to act the way you know is right or to do something wrong—remember "thumbs up." You are Jesus' child, and He will help you do what is right.

Dear Jesus,

I am Your child. I am glad! Amen.

Keep alert and never give up; pray always.
Ephesians 6:18

Rush Here, Rush There

"Hurry up, Catherine," Mother warned. "We have to be moving along."

Catherine was eating breakfast. She stopped looking at the back of the cereal box and started eating faster.

"Catherine, are you coming?" Mother called. "We need to leave now."

Catherine was getting dressed. She stopped playing with her toys and finished putting on her shoes.

"Come on, Catherine," Mother said. "You can't spend all day here."

Catherine had stopped to look at something in the store window.

Did you ever have a day like Catherine's? Someone makes you rush here, rush there. It seems that, on some days, you have to hurry up everywhere.

"Now we don't have to hurry," Catherine's mother said. It was finally nighttime. Now she and her mother had a chance to be together, to pray together. Today, especially, Catherine liked this time. There was nothing to hurry for now!

Dear Jesus,

Sometimes I get too busy. Thanks for always being around to listen when I need to talk. Amen.

Trust in the Lord and you will be happy.
Proverbs 16:20

See What I Can Do!

Instructions: Help your child fill in each blank space. Then act out each sentence together.

I can jump as high as a _____.
I can reach as tall as a _____.
I can hop as far as a _____.
I can take steps as big as a _____.
I can laugh as much as a _____.
I can wink like a _____.
I can wiggle as fast as a _____.
I can smile because _____.

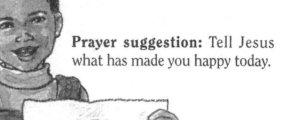

Prayer suggestion: Tell Jesus what has made you happy today.

You made summer and winter.
Psalm 74:16–17.

"It's Not Warm Enough!"

What a beautiful day! The sun was shining. A warm breeze was blowing. Erica thought it was a perfect day to play in the water.

"Mommy, can I put on my swimsuit and run through the hose?" Erica asked.

"No, Erica, it's not warm enough," Mother answered.

"Well, can I fill up the swimming pool?"

"No, Erica, it's not warm enough," Mother said.

"Can I get out the squirt guns and spray water on me?" Erica asked.

What do you think her mother said?

"It's not fun today," Erica said. "You never let me do anything I want."

"Erica, you know that's not true," Mother said. "Let's take down the thermometer and have some fun with it."

Erica's mother put pieces of tape at different temperatures on the outdoor thermometer. On the bottom piece, Mother wrote, "Wear a hat and coat." Another piece of tape, higher up, said, "Wear a jacket." Erica's favorite piece of tape said, "Barefoot, swimsuit."

When will it be warm enough for you to play outside in water? Ask an adult to help you make a thermometer like Erica's.

Dear Jesus,

Sometimes I try to make spring days warmer than they are. Thanks for all kinds of weather. When it gets hot, I know I will want to _____. Amen.

> *The world and all that is in it*
> *belong to the Lord.*
> Psalm 24:1

Keep God's World Beautiful

The sky was getting dark. Thunder began to roll. A few raindrops started to fall. Courtney and Reilly raced inside. "Girls, you look afraid," Courtney's mother said. "What's wrong?"

"It's starting to rain," Reilly said fearfully. "We just talked about dirty rain at school."

"It's terrible, Mommy," Courtney added. "Smoke from chimneys and big trucks goes up to the sky and makes the clouds dirty. Then we get yucky rain."

"God never should've made rain," Reilly said. "That polluted rain can hurt us and fish and my flowers and ..."

"Wait a minute, Reilly," Courtney's mother said. "It's not God's fault we have dirty rain. We just haven't been careful with the nice world God made for us."

Reilly and Courtney were quiet for a minute. They remembered the Bible story about when God created the world. It must have been beautiful.

"You can help make the world a better place, girls," Courtney's mother said gently. "Can you think how?"

Reilly looked outside the window. There was the ice-cream-bar paper she had left in the yard. She would clean that up when the rain stopped.

Courtney thought of something she could do, too. What could Courtney do to help keep God's world beautiful?

Dear Jesus,
Help me remember to keep Your world a nice place to live. Amen.

God loved the world so much
that He gave His only Son.
John 3:16

What Comes First?

Think of what comes first in these actions, then fill in the blanks.

We need a tissue before we blow our _____ .

We need to put on our socks before we put on our

_____ .

We put the cereal in the bowl before we _____ .

Jesus died on a cross before we could go to _____

_____ .

This last sentence is really important.

If it hadn't been for Jesus, we never could have _____

_____ .

Prayer suggestion: Thank Jesus for loving you so that you could love Him back.

*Remember your Creator
while you are still young.*
Ecclesiastes 12:1

The Original Helmet

It was so warm today, Elizabeth could hardly believe it was still spring. As she rode in the car with her dad, the air rushed through the open window and cooled her sweaty hair.

Her dad was driving past a construction site. Many people were working hard; most wore hard hats. "Those workers must really be hot," Elizabeth said. "Their heads must really be sweating."

A sudden noise outside the car window brought a zooming motorcycle next to the car. "That driver's wearing a helmet, too," Elizabeth said excitedly.

"Lots of people wear protective head coverings," Dad said.

Who else wears something to protect his head?

"Of course," Dad added, "God made us the best helmet of all. He made our skulls to cover the soft brain parts in our head. That was a great idea."

"God does have lots of good ideas," agreed Elizabeth.

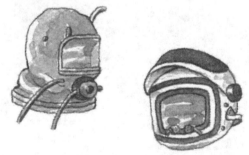

Dear Jesus,

Thanks for all the wonderful things You do. I know the best thing You did for me was to have Jesus die so that my sins would be forgiven. Amen.

Give thanks to the greatest of all gods;
His love is eternal.
Psalm 136:1–3

A Present That's Not Wrapped

April was very excited. One of her favorite people, Nana, was coming to visit. Nana hadn't sent April a birthday present this year, but maybe Nana would bring it along today.

There she was!

"Nana, Nana," April threw her arms around Nana. "I'm so glad you're here."

"How big you are!" Nana said. "You're not my little baby any more. You're a big girl."

"What did you get me, Nana?" April asked. "What did you buy me for my birthday?"

Nana's smile faded.

"Oh, April, I forgot your present," Nana said. "I'm so sorry."

April was so disappointed, she almost started to cry. Nana knelt beside April. She put her arm around her.

"I'm very sorry that I don't have a present all wrapped up for you," Nana said. "But while I'm visiting, I'll try to give you a different kind of gift. I'll spend lots of time with you. We'll go on some walks together, and I'll read a bunch of stories to you."

April looked up. "You know, Nana," April said, "a present doesn't have to be in a box."

Dear Jesus,
    Thank You for Your special gift of love. Amen.

The righteous will flourish like palm trees.
Psalm 92:12–14

Seein' Green

Look out your window. During late spring, many growing things turn a beautiful green color. Find eight things that are green.

Now look inside your house. Can you find eight things inside that are green?

Sometimes people don't think about the color green, but they can't forget it at this beautiful time of year. This lovely color is one of the things of life God has given us to enjoy.

Spring—what a great time to enjoy the color green! What a great time also to enjoy the life God gives each of us.

Dear Jesus,

Thank You for the spring gift of new life outside. Thanks, too, for letting me live in Your colorful world. Amen.

There are many rooms in My Father's house.
John 14:2

Balloons in Heaven?

"Hang onto that balloon, C. J.," Mommy cautioned. "A helium balloon will fly away if you let it go."

"Mommy, if I let the balloon go, would it go all the way to heaven?" C. J. asked.

"It would go far into the sky," Mommy answered.

"But would it go to Grandpa in heaven?" C. J. asked again.

"I'm sure Grandpa is very happy being with Jesus," Mommy said. "He probably doesn't need a green balloon."

"Will they have a birthday cake for Grandpa?" C. J. asked. "Will they know that his favorites are chocolate cake and chocolate frosting?"

"C. J.," Mommy replied, "Grandpa doesn't need a birthday cake in heaven."

"Well, I think he wants a green balloon," said C. J. "I always liked sharing with Grandpa."

C. J. let go of her balloon. She and her mother watched the green balloon sail up to the sky.

That night, C. J. and her mother talked more about heaven. Her mother read John 14:1–4, which talks about heaven.

Dear Jesus,

Thank You for the place in heaven that is waiting for me. Amen.

*Who is it that feeds the ravens
when they wander about hungry?*
Job 38:39–39:1

Thanks, God, for Goldfish

Instructions: Act out this story together.

Amber was so excited! They were going to pick up her new dog. She had been counting the days, and this was it.

Amber cuddled her puppy all the way home in the car. It was so soft, so little! That night, though, Amber had a runny nose.

The next day Amber played with her new puppy whenever it wasn't sound asleep. That night, though, Amber's eyes started to get red. Her nose was still very sniffly.

Amber loved her puppy more and more. And her sniffles got worse and worse. The doctor said she was allergic to her new dog. They would have to give it away.

Amber cried and cried. Even when they found a friend who would love and care for the puppy, Amber was unhappy. Amber's daddy said she could get another pet, but Amber wasn't sure she could love a different pet.

It was a horrible week at Amber's house. Then on Friday night, this was Amber's bedtime prayer:

Thanks, God, for goldfish.

Amber felt better now that she would have a pet that didn't cause allergy problems. What kind of pet do you think Amber got?

Dear Jesus,

Thank You for so many different animals. For animals I see outside the window, like _____. For animals I see at the zoo, like _____ . And for animals I can play with, like _____. Amen.

Christ has been raised from death.
1 Corinthians 15:20

All Gone

Midori and Akeno had loved watching the grass grow longer and greener. It was exciting to see how plants grew bigger. What have you liked about this spring?

One thing made Midori and Akeno sad, though. The bird's nest they had watched with excitement was now empty. The little birds had grown up and gone away. When Akeno looked at the empty nest, he felt empty inside, too.

"Being empty is sometimes good," Mother said. "Remember when you couldn't wait to have the first empty space in your mouth, Akeno?"

"When I lost my tooth!" Akeno remembered.

"And you know how exciting it is to empty your toy box," Mother reminded them. "Empty isn't always bad."

"And in Sunday school, we sing happy songs about the empty tomb on Easter," Midori said. "Empty was good on Easter."

"And an empty nest is a good sign, too," Mother said. "Those two little birds have grown up enough to take care of themselves."

Will you have fun dumping out buckets of sand at a beach this summer? Has your shoe ever felt better after you emptied out some rocks? Think of times when "empty" has been good.

An empty tomb at Easter was a great thing for us all. That meant Jesus had risen. Hallelujah!

Prayer suggestion: Say a thank-You prayer to Jesus.

He showed me Jerusalem.
Revelation 21:10–21

Magic Carpets

"Rain, rain, go away ..." the children said. It had rained for three days. They couldn't play outside. They were bored.

"What can we do?" Mari Jean asked her dad. "There's nothing at all to do."

Her dad thought for a moment. "We'll go to far-off lands," he said with a smile. "We'll take a magic carpet ride!"

Mari Jean and her brother helped her dad put the sofa cushions on the living room floor. They scattered chair cushions in different places, too.

The children ran to their bedrooms and packed for the trip. This was going to be fun!

Everybody found a "magic carpet." They sat on their pillow and told where they were going. Then, when the timer rang five minutes later, they climbed onto another magic carpet and went to a different place.

"I'm going to an island this time," Mari Jean announced. "It's a good thing I brought my crayons."

"I'm going to look for penguins," said her brother. He was looking at his book about polar bears and birds of the Arctic.

"I'm going up to heaven," their dad said. "I just want to look around. Have a great trip you two."

If you could go on a magic carpet ride to heaven, whom would you visit? What would you see? You can read about heaven in Revelation 21:10–21.

Prayer suggestion: Talk to Jesus about heaven.

Leave all your worries with Him.
1 Peter 5:6–7

Worried?

Everybody was having fun, splashing in the water. Splash! Whoosh! Everybody was having fun. Everybody except Kayla. She just sat in a chair by the pool. Her swimsuit wasn't even wet.

"What's wrong with Kayla?" Kelly asked.

"Just leave her alone," somebody answered.

"She's so crabby she's not fun anyway," another one said.

Kayla still just sat there.

"What's wrong?" Kelly asked.

"Nothing," said Kayla.

"Something must be wrong," Kelly said. "You're never like this, all sad and frowny."

"My mom's in the hospital," Kayla explained. "I saw her yesterday, and she didn't look like she used to."

"What was she doing?" Kelly asked.

"She was just lying in a bed," Kayla said. "I never saw her just lying in a bed at lunchtime. It was scary."

Have you ever visited a hospital? Talk to someone about what you saw. When you know about a hospital, it won't seem so scary.

Dear Jesus,

Thank You for doctors and nurses and all the other people who work at hospitals to help people feel better. Amen.

Pray at all times.
1 Thessalonians 5:16–18

"I'm So Tired!"

It had been a long day for Sara. She couldn't wait to crawl into bed. Off came the shoes; next the clothes. Then the pajamas went on.

"I'm too tired to brush my teeth," Sara complained.

"Okay," said Dad. "Just this once."

"I'm too tired to pick up the things in my room," Sara said.

"Okay, you can do it in the morning," Dad said.

"I'm too tired to pray," said Sara.

"No, Sara, that's not something we skip," Dad said. "God gave us this wonderfully busy day. We can at least say thank You."

This was Sara's prayer:

Dear Jesus,
  when You were little, I think You got tired just like I am. Thank You for this wonderful day. Amen.

And Sara fell right to sleep.

Have you ever had such a busy day that you wanted to skip talking to Jesus? Jesus will listen to a short prayer or a long prayer. He just likes to listen to what you say.

Prayer suggestion: Talk to Jesus about your day.

Always give thanks for everything to God.
Ephesians 5:20

Snack on a Stick

Instructions: Ask your child to make a growling sound each time you read, "Peter's stomach rumbled."

"Hey, Dad," Peter said. "We're all hungry." *Peter's stomach rumbled.*

"It's not time for lunch, guys," Dad said.

"But we're starved," Peter said. *Peter's stomach rumbled.*

"Okay," Dad said. "I'll see what I can come up with."

Pretty soon Dad came out of the house carrying a tray. "Find some thin sticks, guys, and peel off the bark," he said. *Peter's stomach rumbled.*

"Dad, we can't eat sticks," Peter said. *Peter's stomach rumbled.*

"Of course not," said Dad. "But we're just starting off the summer fruit season, and here's your first stick-snack of the year. Now, watch what I do." *Peter's stomach rumbled.*

Dad took a melon ball from the tray and stuck it all the way to the end of a peeled stick. Then he did the same with a big strawberry and a grape. Soon the whole stick was covered with fresh fruit. *Peter's stomach rumbled.*

"That's a summer stick-snack, guys," Dad explained. "Now, let's pray together and then dig in."

"Pray?" one of Peter's friends asked. "It's not bedtime."

"We always give thanks for our food," Peter's dad said. "These are fruits we haven't enjoyed since last summer; let's thank God for giving us such a wonderful snack.

Prayer suggestion: Thank God for your favorite summer foods.

Their father loved Joseph.
Genesis 37:4

Joe and His Coat

Colin was going to a puppet show. Actually, his mother had explained, there would be several shows. Children at church had worked on making puppets, a stage, and even had written the words their puppets would say. Colin had never been to a puppet show. This would be fun.

Colin thought the puppets were great. His favorite show was "Joe and His Coat." The story had been about a boy, Joseph, whose father gave him a coat. "Thanks, Dad," Puppet Joe said. "The colors match my sandals." Colin had laughed at Puppet Joe.

When Colin got home, he wanted to do a puppet show, too. The back of the sofa would be a great stage. But where could he find a good story for puppets?

"Try the Bible," Mother suggested.

"The Bible is just for big people," Colin said.

"Most of the stories you hear at church are from the Bible," Mother said. "That puppet show you liked best today, 'Joe and His Coat,' was from the Bible."

Colin and his mother sat down with the Bible. Colin couldn't read yet, but his mother read Genesis 37:1–11, the story of Joseph.

What Bible story could you make into a puppet show? Ask an adult to help you.

Dear Jesus,

I know You loved Joseph. You took care of him. I know You love me. You will take care of me, too. Amen.

Friends always show their love.
Proverbs 17:17

A Ducky Day!

Orlanda and her mother were feeding the ducks at the park. Other children were, too. Orlanda smiled at someone, but then Orlanda looked puzzled. Orlando thought that the person who smiled back at her looked different.

"Mommy, what's wrong with that girl's face?" Orlanda asked quietly.

"I'm not sure," Mother answered, "but she might have Down's Syndrome."

"Is that like chicken pox without spots?" Orlanda asked.

"No," said Mother. "It's something that happened to her long before she was born. If that girl has Down's, it just means she will have a harder time learning some things. But she sure knows how to feed the ducks. Look how they follow her."

Orlanda ran over to her new friend and smiled. Maybe Orlanda could learn how to make the ducks follow her, too.

Orlanda and the other girl had a wonderful time that day. Orlanda learned there was only one thing better than feeding ducks—it was feeding ducks with a friend!

Draw a picture of you and a friend having fun.

Dear Jesus,
Thank You for friends to talk to, play with, and learn from. Amen.

*The disciples got into the boat
in which Jesus was already sitting.*
Mark 4:35–39

Alone in a Crowd?

Instructions: Pretend with your child that you are in a boat.

Laurel had looked forward to this boat ride for a long time. Her first time on a real boat! Mommy and Daddy were having a great time talking to their friends. Everybody on the boat seemed happy.

Everybody except Laurel. The gentle bouncing on the waves made her stomach feel dizzy. The bright sun shone on the water, but that made Laurel's eyes hurt. She squinted and looked around. Mommy and Daddy were right there, but she felt all alone. Nobody was paying any attention to her. And besides, she wasn't having fun at all.

Laurel didn't know what to do. What would you have done?

Then Laurel had an idea. She would sing a song from church—just to herself, of course. That might help. Her teacher had said that Jesus is always with us. Maybe if she sang a song, she wouldn't feel so lonesome.

Laurel sang very quietly, just to herself. She started to feel better. Then she whispered another song. This boat ride was getting to be fun.

Laurel's mother looked over at her and smiled. What do you think she told Laurel?

Dear Jesus,

Thank You for always being with me. Sometimes I forget that I always have You as a friend. Amen.

You make ... plants for man to use.
Psalm 104:14–15

Underground Food

Paulo tugged and tugged. The dandelion just wouldn't come up.

"Be sure you get the root," Mother cautioned. "Otherwise, that weed will grow right back again."

"Why did God make plants so they have roots anyway?" Paulo asked. "It just is so hard to weed."

"It's a good thing God made roots for plants," Paulo's mother answered. "You wouldn't have your favorite sweet potato pie without a root. You know, a sweet potato is an underground food."

Miranda, Paulo's older sister, added, "And what about the radishes and carrots we'll be pulling up to eat in a few weeks? You love those foods."

As Paulo pulled out the whole dandelion root, he said with a smile, "Finally! That's one big dandelion gone forever." He threw it into the weed bag.

"Paulo," Mother said, "remember that God always takes care of us, even when our food hides under the ground."

Dear Jesus,
    Thank You for food that grows on trees, like _____
_____. Thank You for food that grows
on top of the ground, like _____.
Thank You for food that grows under the ground, like _____
_____. Amen.

We will always praise You.
Psalm 44:8

Time for Bed

"Drew, time for bed," Dad called. "Brush your teeth."

"Dad, it can't be bedtime already," Drew said. "Everybody else is staying up."

"Drew, it is bedtime for *you*," Dad explained. "Each of you kids has a different bedtime. You each need different amounts of sleep."

"Well, it's just not fair," Drew complained.

"We'll talk about it when I come to pray with you," Dad said. "But now, brush your teeth."

When Drew's dad came into the bedroom for prayers, Drew still had a frown on his face. It was no fun being the youngest, especially at bedtime.

"If I was born first, I could stay up last," Drew pouted.

"That's true," Dad said. "If you were the oldest, you could also cut the grass and help with the shopping."

Drew thought about that. Maybe being littlest in the family wasn't so bad. "Dad, when I get older, will you still tuck me in at night?" Drew asked. "Will you still pray with me?"

"I'll do that as long as you'd like," Dad answered. "Now, let's pray."

Prayer suggestion: Say a prayer thanking God for the things you did today.

The Lord ... [is] the Creator of heaven, earth, and sea.
Psalm 146:5–6

Round and Round

Have you ever been to a fair or park that has things that go round and round? What are some things you can think of that move like that? Take your finger and make circles and circles. That might give you some ideas.

In the summertime, children ride on many kinds of things that go around. What's something that goes around and is high in the air, then low on the ground? What's something that goes around and around very fast? Did you think of things like merry-go-rounds and little racing cars? Those can be a lot of fun.

You're going around right now. You might not feel it, but the earth is turning. Our earth is always going around. God made it that way.

As you get older, you will learn more about how our earth moves. You will learn about other things in our universe that move, too. God has made a wonderful place for us to live. He's created interesting things for us to explore.

God is a wonderful and powerful God. "Creator of the Universe" is one way to describe God. And do you know what? That's exactly right.

Prayer suggestion:
Say a prayer to God as
Creator of the universe.

His Son ... Savior.
John 3:17

Alike and Different

Instructions: Play this game together. As each of you answers the questions, talk about ways you are the same and ways you are different.

What color is your hair?

What is your favorite summer food?

What do you like to do at the beach?

What is your favorite day in the summer months?

Who loves you?

There are lots of ways to answer that last question. But there's one answer you and everyone else can give: God loves you. He loves everyone.

We are all different in some ways. But we are all alike in one way: God loves us. And that's good news for today and every day.

Prayer suggestion: Talk with God now.

You know the way.
John 14:4–6

Map Fun

Instructions: Make a "relief map" together in the sandbox. Build mountains, rivers, and highways.

Andy's dad had been studying the maps for a long time.

"What's a map for?" Andy finally asked.

"A map shows all different places and how to get there," Dad answered. "I'm figuring out the roads we'll take on our vacation."

"What are all those blue places?" Andy asked.

"Blue is for water," Dad answered.

"What about those red lines?" Andy asked next.

"Those are the big highways," Dad replied. "I think we'll be going on one of them for a long way."

"How do we get to Grandma's?" Andy asked. His dad showed him the way.

"How do we get to Uncle Wallace's?" Dad showed him the way.

"How do we get to Disney World?" His dad showed him the way.

"How do we get to heaven?" Andy asked finally.

"That's not on this map," said Dad. "The Bible is our map to heaven."

"I never saw lines and lakes in the Bible," Andy said.

Dad laughed. "In the Bible, Jesus tells us that we need to believe in Him as our Savior, and that's the way to heaven," Dad explained. "That's how the Bible is our map."

Dear Jesus,

I like many places. I always have fun when I go to
_____. I laugh when I go to _____.
Thank You for having a place for me in heaven. Amen.

You will be witnesses for me.
Acts 1:8

Grown-up Jobs

Paige rubbed her hand carefully over the bandage on her arm. It still hurt where she had gotten the shot.

"I'm sure not going to be a doctor when I grow up," Paige told her mother. "Nobody would like you because you give shots."

"Sometimes a person has to hurt in order to help someone else," Mother said. "That sounds strange, but that shot will keep you from getting a terrible illness."

"I still think being a doctor is an icky job—except if you help people have babies," Paige said.

"There are good parts and not-so-good parts about any job," Mother said. "I love my job, but I don't like being away from you so much of the time."

"I'm going to find a job that is fun and everybody likes you," Paige said. She was quiet for a while, just thinking.

"I know!" Paige said. "I'll tell people about Jesus. That's a big job, and everybody wants to hear more about Jesus."

Paige is thinking about when she grows up. But she could tell people about Jesus right now, even though she is still little. So can you. Which of your friends can you talk to about Jesus? Whom can you invite to church?

Prayer suggestion: Talk to God now about how you can tell others about Jesus.

There will always be cold and heat,
summer and winter, day and night.
Genesis 8:22

Why Does the Sun Shine?

"Why does God make the sun shine?" Richard asked.

"So our vegetables will grow in the garden," said Mom.

"Why else?" asked Richard.

"So I can cut the grass with the new mower," said Mom.

"Why else?" asked Richard.

"So it looks like a perfect summer day," said Mom.

"But why else does God make the sun shine?" Richard asked.

"I just don't know," said Mom.

"So I can wear my new swimsuit and lie in the sun on my new beach towel," said Richard. "That's why God makes the sun shine!"

"That's a very good reason," said Mom.

Did the sun shine at your house today? How would you describe the weather where you live?

Dear God,

Thank You for all sorts of days. For the gentle rain that helps the flowers grow. For the wind that blows the seeds around to start new plants. And for the bright, sunny summer days. Thanks, God, for always smiling at me. Amen.

Help carry one another's burdens.
Galatians 6:2

A Good Kind of Tired

"Daddy, why are you so tired after work?" Chona asked.

"I have a 'feeling job,' Chona," Daddy answered. "That makes me very tired."

"What does that mean, Daddy?" Chona asked. "Do you touch people who come to your office?"

Her father laughed. He explained that a counselor tries to help people with their problems. People can come and talk to him about things they need help with; then he listens. He feels their problems almost as though they were his own. Sometimes he can help.

"Ana's mother is tired after work, too," Chona said. "She helps people, too."

Chona was quiet for a moment. She was thinking of some other helping people. Whom can you think of?

"It's a good kind of tired, though," Chona's father said. "I feel happy inside that I can help people."

"Pastor Martin must feel a good kind of tired, too," said Chona. "He helps people all the time."

Chona was right about her pastor. Does your minister feel a good kind of tired from helping people? Does he like telling people about Jesus?

Ask your pastor about his job. Maybe you will have a "feeling job" when you grow up.

Dear Jesus,

Thank You for these people who tell me about Jesus: _____ . Amen.

God sent the Spirit of His Son into our hearts.
Galatians 4:4–7

Half and Half

"I just got a new dog," said Rudi. "He's half beagle and half something else."

"My dog is part pointer and part Lab," said Suvi.

Tara was quiet. She didn't have a dog. She didn't have a cat or any pet.

Then she had a great idea. "I'm part my mom's and part Jesus' child," Tara said. "Half and half make a whole—so that's me!"

Tara was trying to explain whose child she was. How would you explain whose child you are?

Dear Jesus,
I like being Your child. Amen.

Let us go to the Lord's house.
Psalm 122:1

A Special Friend

Instructions: Act out the italicized words in this story together.

Today was a special day for Anna. Her friend Evelyn had invited her to watch *baton twirling* practice.

Anna felt so grown up. Evelyn was a teenager. She helped teach Anna's class at Sunday school. Anna liked Evelyn so much. Sometimes Evelyn baby-sat for Anna. Now Anna could watch Evelyn practice for *marching in a parade*.

Evelyn started practicing by *lying on the ground*. Anna thought that was funny, but Evelyn said that baton twirlers first must *stretch* their bodies. Then she *jogged*.

When Evelyn finished warming up, she took the baton and tried some *twirls, circles*, and *spins* from the routine she would do during the parade. Anna thought Evelyn was beautiful, even without a pretty costume.

"Evelyn, when I grow up, I want to be just like you," Anna said. "I want to go to the same school, take *twirling* lessons, and everything!"

Evelyn said, "You'll be your very own person, Anna. I'm glad you want to be like me, but you'll be you. And that's nice, too."

Anna was quiet for a minute. Then she had an idea. "Well, at least we can still go to the same church together!"

What friends do you see at church?

Dear Jesus,
Thank You for letting me go to a church where I can see my friends and learn about You. Amen.

I will be with you always.
Matthew 28:20

Moving Around

Moving your body can be fun. Can you move an ankle? Now move your heel. Now move your elbow. Moving *can* be fun!

But when you move your body from your house in your town to another house in another town and never move back, that's hard. A moving van can carry your toys, books, even the refrigerator, but your friends can't go with you. You can't move a favorite tree or even the view you see from your bedroom. That's when moving is hard.

But Jesus is always with you. He's with you when you move your body for fun—when you move your hands or your feet or your tummy. He's with you when it's hard to move to another place to live. You never have to pack Jesus. He'll move right along with you.

Dear Jesus,

Thank You for always being with me. When I move from place to place or when I just move me, I know You're there. Amen.

The Lord will protect you.
Psalm 121:7–8

My Home

Instructions: Help your child answer these riddles.

Goldfish swim in a _____. (bowl)

A gopher digs a deep _____. (hole)

A bat flies into a _____. (cave)

A whale swims over a _____. (wave)

A snail carries his _____. (house)

A trap is not a good place for a _____. (mouse)

A pig lives in a _____. (pen)

A bear lives in a _____. (den)

A bird lives in a _____. (nest)

But where I live is the _____! (best)

Dear Jesus,

Thank You for giving me a place to live. Sometimes I forget to thank You for that. My favorite thing about where I live is _____ . Amen.

God ... loved us.
1 John 4:10–11

A Good Game?

Do you ever talk like this with your friends?

Ashlie: "I can zipper."

Dillon: "Well, I can tie."

Ashlie: "I could button when I was two years old."

Dillon: "When I was born, I could do that."

Dillon and Ashlie are playing a game that isn't much fun. Adults call it one-upmanship. People try to say things that will make them feel they are better than another person. Nobody wins at that game, and everybody starts to feel bad.

Some people foolishly think, "Jesus loves me better than you." *That's not true.* Jesus loves everyone just the same, and *more* than they know. Jesus died on the cross for everybody.

The special thing about Jesus is that He's not playing a game. Jesus is for real. And that can make us all feel so good!

Dear Jesus,

It's not easy always being nice. Help me to show the kind of love that You showed when You died for me. Amen.

Every year the parents of Jesus went to Jerusalem.
Luke 2:41

It's Always Hot

"My, you have hot summers here," Grandma said to Erin.

"We have hot everything," Erin said. "It's sweating hot in summer. Even at Christmas it's warm."

"We sure could use some of your warm weather up where I live," Grandma said. "It's so cold that sometimes I don't even want to take out the garbage."

Where do you think Erin's grandma lives? Do different seasons cause weather changes where you live?

"I wish I lived where you live, Grandma," Erin said. "It's always the same here."

"Well, Erin, God made a wonderful place when He created earth," Grandma said. "Some places stay much the same all year. That's how it is where Jesus lived."

"Really, Grandma?" Erin asked. "You mean, Jesus always had hot feet too?"

"Well, I can't say for sure," Grandma said. "But most days, the little boy Jesus probably had weather much like the little girl Erin."

Erin was quiet. It was exciting to think that Jesus was her age once. She wondered about the school Jesus went to.

If you want to read about Jesus when He was a little boy, look in Luke 2:41–52.

Dear Jesus,

It's good to remember that You started out as a child, just like me. You know what it's like to be _____ years old. Amen.

Being wise is better than being strong.
Proverbs 24:5

Keeping Cool

"Oooh," Lynn said. "Look at that pig!"

A great big pig was almost swimming in mud. It plopped on one side and then turned over to cover the rest of its body in mud.

"Yuck," said Lynn, "I'm glad I'm not a pig. Mrs. Harris, why do they like to get so dirty?" Mrs. Harris was a farmer.

"I'm not sure pigs like to get dirty," Mrs. Harris said. "But wallowing in mud helps the pigs stay cool on hot days like this.

"Pigs don't sweat; they don't perspire like we do to keep cool on days like this," she continued. "Also, mud won't let them get sunburned."

Lynn laughed. She couldn't imagine a sunburned pig.

"Mud also protects pigs from getting bitten by lots of insects," Mrs. Harris added.

"I never knew pigs were so smart," Lynn said. "That's a really good idea."

"Actually, God takes care of pigs just like He cares for everything else on this farm," Mrs. Harris said.

"He takes better care of me," Lynn said. "I don't have to roll in mud to keep cool!"

Dear Jesus,

I know You taught birds how to make nests and pigs how to keep cool. Thank You for helping people a long time ago write the Bible so that I know about You. That's most important of all. Amen.

You made summer.
Psalm 74:16–17

Summer Sillies

Instructions: Act out the italicized words with your child.

Billie Jo was sweating. It was terribly hot. She hated summer.

"I'm tired of this weather," she complained to her mother. "There's nothing to do but get hot."

"It's time to play a game," said Mother. "Let's think of all the things we can do just in summer."

Billie Jo watched in amazement as her mother stood up and started *marching around* the kitchen.

"What are you doing?" Billie Jo asked.

"I'm marching in a parade," Mother answered. "Remember what fun you had the other day *carrying a flag*? You couldn't do that in winter."

Mother sat down and *licked the air*. What do you think Billie Jo's mother was acting out now?

"You're eating an ice-cream cone," Billie Jo said. "I don't believe it, though, Mommy. You never act silly like this."

"That's one of the fun things about summer," Mother said, smiling. "Summer sillies are great fun for everybody."

Billie Jo smiled. Maybe summer wasn't so bad!

What can you act out that you do only in summer? Ask the person reading this book to act out something, too. And have fun. It's summer, one of God's great times of the year.

Dear Jesus,

Thank You for the summertime, a time when I can do all kinds of things, like _____. Amen.

Isn't He the carpenter's son?
Matthew 13:55

A Good Helper

Curt knew today would be really hot. Breakfast was barely over, and already the sun was burning. There wasn't a cloud in the sky. What a day to have to work outside with his dad!

Curt and his dad collected the tools they needed. They would be weeding the garden, trimming the bushes, and cleaning out the flower beds. What kinds of tools did they take outside?

Curt liked to be with his dad. He just wished the weather wasn't so hot. Sweat dripped down Curt's face. His hands were filthy from working in the mud. Every time he tried to clean his face, it got dirtier.

Then Curt and his dad went inside to get some cold water. His dad smiled.

"This is tough work," Dad said. "But you're a great help. I'm sure Joseph was just as glad to have help in the carpentry shop a long time ago."

Curt smiled. It felt good that Dad needed him. He'd work even harder now. But Joseph? They didn't know a Joseph who was a carpenter.

Then Curt smiled again. He remembered whom his dad was talking about. Do you know?

Dear Jesus,
Thank You for the chance to be with people who help us work. Amen.

Pray at all times.
1 Thessalonians 5:16–18

No Lights!

The thunder crashed and the lightning crackled. Suddenly the TV blinked off. The lights in the living room went off, too. Michael tried the kitchen lights. Nothing happened. Dad tried to call the electric company. The phone didn't work.

"The storm knocked down wires somewhere," Dad said.

"What can we do?" Michael asked.

"We'll wait until things get fixed," Dad answered. "Meanwhile, let's see what still works."

"We can play my radio," Michael said. "It has batteries."

"The cuckoo clock still works," Michael's uncle said. "I know it's near supper, so I'll fix some sandwiches."

Soon the family gathered around the supper table. The lights still hadn't come on. The phone still didn't work.

"At least we can pray," Michael said. "Jesus still works!"

Walk around your house and see what is electrically powered. What would still work if the electricity went off?

Dear Jesus,

I know You are always with me. When I'm scared or afraid, I can always talk to You. I can tell You about things that make me happy, too. Thank You, Jesus, for being You. Amen.

God's message is near you,
on your lips and in your heart.
Romans 10:8

"Pack Up—Let's Go!"

Her vacation was getting closer and closer. Finally, packing day arrived.

"Let's think from head to toe," Daddy said. "That way we won't miss anything you'll need."

For her head, she'll pack _____.

For her body, she'll pack _____.

For her feet, she'll pack _____.

Pack Christa's beach bag, too.

For her head, she'll pack _____.

For her body, she'll pack _____.

For her feet, she'll pack _____.

Did you remember the suntan lotion?

Christa and her dad closed the suitcase. Then they zipped the beach bag.

"But, Daddy, we forgot something," Christa said. "We forgot the book we use to talk to Jesus every night. And I don't know where to pack it. It's not part of my head or my body or my feet."

"Put the book in the car with the maps," Daddy said. "That way we'll be sure to remember to take *Little Visits with Jesus* along. But Jesus Himself lives in your heart."

Jesus lives in your heart, too. How does that make you feel?

Prayer suggestion: Tell Jesus how it feels to have Him living in your heart.

A Thank-You Day

Sandy snuggled deeper under the covers. Outside the bedroom, she could hear the storm. Thunder crashed. Lightning flashed. Even though it was the middle of the night, the lightning made the sky seem bright.

Then Sandy remembered—she had left her brand-new, red fire truck outside. Quickly she got out of bed and turned on the bedroom light—and saw her truck sitting on her dresser. Someone had brought it in for her. What a relief! Sandy turned the light off and jumped back into bed.

The next day, Sandy was extra nice to everybody. She did not know who had saved her truck from the storm, so she would help everyone as a thank you. She helped her mom tie up the tomato plants. She helped her brother sweep the garage. Sandy even helped take out the smelly garbage.

At bedtime, Sandy remembered the nice day. She felt good about being helpful. This was her prayer:

Dear Jesus, I feel happy as I talk to You tonight. I feel so good inside me. I wonder if that's how You felt when You died on the cross. I know it couldn't have been nice, but I think You felt good inside. Well, it's time to go to sleep. Talk to You tomorrow, Jesus.

How do you feel after hearing Sandy's prayer?

Prayer suggestion: Ask Jesus to help you make tomorrow a thank-you day for people you love.

Who can tell all the great things He has done?
Psalm 106:1–2

A Mud-Cake Party

Jamie and Kami were having a great time. First they mixed up some mud. The mud was cool, wet, and, oh, so muddy. Then they put it in a leftover egg carton and let the mud dry. Soon they would have mud cakes!

Later they checked on their baking. Yes, the mud cakes were almost done. Carefully they turned over the egg carton and—plop—out fell the mud cakes.

The girls were just setting up a pretend party when Kami's mother came out.

"What are you two doing?" Mother asked.

"We're having a mud-cake party," Kami said happily.

"How in the world did you get so messy?" Mother asked.

"When God made mud, He made it messy," Jamie replied.

What do you think Mother said?

Dear Jesus,

Thanks for all the things in this world I can have fun with. When I look under a rock, I might find _____ _____. When I climb a tree, I might see _____. And when I play in mud, _____. Amen.

147

Your word is a lamp to guide me.
Psalm 119:105

"When Will I Read?"

"Mommy, when will I read?"

Have you ever asked that question? Pretend to take a book off a shelf. Now open it. Pretend you are reading.

Even if you can't read words, all the things you just acted out are part of learning to read. You know how to hold a book and open it. You know that you start at the beginning of a book. You know that a book goes from the front to the back. All those things are part of getting ready to read.

Next time you go outside, look for a stop sign. I'll bet you already know what color it is and that it says, "Stop." You *are* learning how to read.

It won't be long before you read your own name or pick out words you know in a book.

Before long, you'll be reading really big books—all by yourself. Even the Bible. But for now, ask someone to read your favorite Bible story to you.

Dear Jesus,

Thank You for all the good stories in the Bible. I really like the story of _____ . Amen.

I will proclaim Your greatness, my God and King.
Psalm 145:1–3

A Sit-Down Summer

Instructions: Act out this devotion with your child.

Andrew felt terrible. It was only the middle of the summer, and he had a broken leg. No more swimming and no more riding his bike. And for at least a week, he'd have to have his leg propped up. What could he do for a whole week sitting down? What are some things you might do?

At first, Andrew only looked out the window. That was not fun. Next he watched television. That got very boring.

Then his mother had an idea. "Andrew, if you think only about yourself all the time, the days will seem to go slowly. Why don't you do things for people?" she suggested. "I'll call Mrs. White. She loves to have you sit and tell her about what it's like to be your age."

"Okay," said Andrew, but not very happily.

"Tomorrow you can work for the church bazaar," Mother added. "You can sort yarn and count squares."

"And the next day will be even busier," Mother continued. "That's when I visit people at the nursing home. Do you think you can draw pictures to take to everybody? Maybe you can use a wheelchair to deliver your pictures."

"Can I use colored chalk, too?" Andrew said with a little eagerness. "That makes nice summer pictures."

"Of course," said Mother. "A sit-down summer might not be as great as a walking one, but we'll make it good anyway."

Prayer suggestion: When you talk to God today, thank Him for all the things you can walk to and for your wonderful legs.

Whoever believes in Me will live,
even though he dies.
John 11:25–26.

A Special Reminder

Cathy had spent three wonderful weeks with her grandparents and great-aunt Hulda. She liked being with her grandma and grandpa, but most of all, Cathy enjoyed her great-aunt Hulda. Her great-aunt Hulda was very old. Her hair was white; her hands had purple lines. She couldn't hear very well. But Cathy and Great-aunt Hulda had become special friends.

Now it was time for Cathy to go home. Everyone had said good-bye—except Cathy and Great-aunt Hulda. How do you think Cathy feels?

"I wish I could stay with you," Cathy said. "I love you."

"For you," Great-aunt Hulda said. It was the lace bookmark from her Bible. She hugged Cathy one last time.

As Cathy rode away in the car, she waved to everyone. There were Grandma and Grandpa and Great-aunt Hulda sitting on the porch. As always, her Bible lay open on Great-aunt Hulda's lap.

Cathy held tight to the bookmark. She would always remember how special the Bible bookmark was to Great-aunt Hulda. Now it would be very special to Cathy.

Great-aunt Hulda died soon after summer ended. Cathy was glad *and* sad. Why do you think Cathy felt like that?

Dear Jesus,

When I think about someone dying, I feel _____ _____. Thank You for giving me people I can talk to about dying. Help me remember I can always talk to You. Amen.

Your constant love reaches above the heavens.
Psalm 108:4

Playing Statues

John thought this building was his favorite of the whole vacation. He went from room to room. Every room had lots to look at. Most rooms had paintings. Some rooms had furniture. But John's favorite thing in this whole place was a statue. Actually, he liked a lot of the statues. Can you guess where John was?

When John got back to the motel, he played "statues." He remembered the poses of some of the statues he had seen at the art museum. Play statues with John.

Be a happy statue. Now freeze ... don't move! Be a tired statue. Now freeze ... don't move. Next be a statue that has just discovered a secret. Now freeze ... don't move. Be a statue of Jesus. Now *move*. Show something Jesus would do.

Dear Jesus,

Thank You that I can feel and look many different ways. Most of all, I am thankful for You. I am also thankful for _____

_____.

Amen.

Lord, You have made so many things!
Psalm 104:24

Twinkling Christmas Lights

Cary was so excited! Visiting her cousin was great, but tonight would be the best of all. Cary was going to look for fireflies. She didn't have any fireflies where she lived.

Sure enough, when it started to get dark, Cary looked out the window and saw little dots of light blink on and off. It was time. She got the margarine container that had been washed out. Earlier, she had poked tiny holes in the lid.

Now Cary and her cousin raced around the lawn. There! She caught one. Now another. This was a lot of fun.

"Girls, time to come in," Cary's aunt called.

Cary looked down at the container. Every so often, one of those little fireflies would blink on a friendly "hello." Cary carefully opened the lid and let them fly out. How brightly they fluttered away—just like Christmas lights!

Cary had a special prayer for God that night. She said,

Thank You, God, for tonight. Now that I'm big,
I think I know lots of things. But until today,
I didn't know about Your special fireflies.
Thank You for surprising me. Amen.

Has something in God's wonderful world ever surprised you? See what you can learn about fireflies. Are they really flies? How do they light up?

If you can't find the answers, here they are: Fireflies are not really flies at all. A firefly is really a beetle. To make light, the oxygen that the firefly breathes combines with chemicals in a special "light organ" underneath the firefly.

Prayer suggestion: Talk to God about an animal, insect, bird, or fish that you think is special.

How good it is to give thanks to You, O Lord.
Psalm 92:1

Flying High

Jan heard the noise: "Sh-sh-sh."

"Sh-sh-sh." There it was again. It seemed to come from up above. "Sh-sh-whoosh!" What was that? Jan ran out from under the trees. Now she could see the sky. What was making that noise?

"Sh-sh-whoosh!" Jan saw a beautiful, giant balloon. It was so low that Jan could see three people in the basket underneath. Jan waved.

"Sh-sh-whoosh-sh!" There went the balloon, floating over other houses, past other trees. What a thrill! Jan watched until the balloon was just a dot in the sky.

What a special summer day.

Dear Jesus,

Every day, I thank You for food and people who love me. Every day, I thank You for a place to live and a church to go to. Today, I want to thank You for the special things of summer. Thank You for _____. Amen.

God loves the one who gives gladly.
2 Corinthians 9:7–8

$$$$$$

"Wow! Thanks for the money, Grandpa," Robert said. He took the new quarter right to his bank. Then he opened the hole in the bottom of the bank and shook out all his money. There was a lot. Robert carefully sorted all the money into little stacks. He turned over each coin to see who was pictured.

"Who is this?" Robert held up a quarter. His grandfather said it was a famous person.

"Who is this?" Robert held up a dime. Whose picture is on a dime?

"Who is on a penny?" Robert asked next. Do you know?

Robert looked at all the famous people on his money. He was puzzled. One famous person was missing. "Grandpa, Jesus is famous," Robert said. "Why isn't His picture on money?"

"Jesus could be on money, I guess," Grandpa answered. "But His picture would need to be on money for every country in the world.

"Our money shows famous people from our country," Grandpa said. "Jesus is important to people in all the countries of the world."

Can you draw a picture of a bill or coin with Jesus' picture on it? Could your picture be used as money anywhere on earth?

Dear Jesus,

I like money. I like to count it. I like to save it. I like to spend it. Please help me remember to share it with You and with people who need it. Amen.

I love you.
John 15:9

Listen to Love

We hear many different sounds. Let's play a listening game.

Make a soft sound.

Make a squeaky sound.

Make a sound without using your voice.

I think the sound of love is beautiful. Well ... maybe I can't hear love, but I can hear what love does. I heard love yesterday when a child told me, "I'm sorry."

This morning, I heard a little boy comfort another boy who fell down. He said, "Let's go inside and get a bandage." That was a nice sound of love.

Jesus says the words, "I love you." That's a beautiful sound. If you are ever hurt or tired or angry, look in the Bible for Jesus' words. His "I love you" sounds so good!

Read Jesus' words in John 15:9. Then put a bookmark at that page. When you are feeling bad, you can open the Bible to those words. Even if you don't know how to read, you can know that Jesus says, "I love you."

Prayer suggestion: Say an "I love You" prayer to Jesus.

155

The water which had come together
He named "Sea."
Genesis 1:9–10

Water, Water Everywhere

What a hot day! Anne was really sweating. She couldn't wait to get inside for a glass of water.

"I'm home, Mom," she called as she walked right to the sink. Nothing came out of the faucet.

She went to the bathroom and turned on that faucet. That didn't work either.

"Mom, there's no water," she called.

"The plumber's here fixing a leak," Mother answered. "The water is turned off all over the house."

What could Anne do? When Anne said her bed-time prayers, she thanked God for something very important. Anne used it every day but had never said a word of thanks for it before. What did Anne give thanks for that night?

Dear Jesus,

Sometimes I forget to thank You for things that don't seem so important—until I don't have them. Tonight I want to thank You for water. Water tastes especially good to me when _____ . Water is lots of fun when _____ . I know I was baptized with water, too. That's most special of all. Amen.

Ever since you were a child,
you have known the Holy Scriptures.
2 Timothy 3:15

Make a "Good Book"

"It's too hot," Mimi complained.

"Yes," said Father, "it's very hot."

"I'm too hot outside," said Mimi. "I'm too hot inside. There's nothing to do."

"When I'm bored, I work in the basement," said Father. "Why don't you get out those scrap pieces of wood I gave you?"

"No," said Mimi, "it's too hot to hammer."

"When I want something to do," Mimi's mother said, "I get out the sewing kit. Why don't you get out those pretty pieces of material I gave you for doll clothes?"

"No," said Mimi, "my dolls would be too hot all dressed up today."

Her grandma said, "Mimi, when I have a spare minute, I pick up my Bible and read."

"But I can't read words," said Mimi.

"Make your own 'Good Book,' " said Grandma. "Draw pictures of your favorite Bible stories. Then I'll help you put them together into a real book."

That's what Mimi worked on for the rest of the day. What Bible stories do you think she drew? Can you make your own "Good Book"?

Dear Jesus,

Thank You for time to do many different kinds of things. Amen.

All living things look hopefully to You.
Psalm 145:13–16

A Smelly Hike

Willie was enjoying his first nature walk. The woods were nice and cool. Everything was quiet. The group hadn't seen a snake— yet. Willie was afraid he might get scared of that. But best of all, his nature bag was almost full.

Willie had found something thinner than a pencil. What do you think he found?

Willie had found something that would reflect the sun. What was that?

Willie had found something that was his favorite color—green. What green thing did Willie put in his nature bag?

But what was that awful smell? "There was a skunk around here, folks," the hike leader said. "Can you smell that? It's the best way a skunk has to protect itself. A skunk doesn't run very fast or climb very well. It just squirts a liquid to keep enemies away."

"But it smells terrible!" Willie said.

"Yes," the leader said, "but God gave each animal a special way to take care of itself. That liquid the skunk sprays is a pretty good protector."

God made each animal special, but He made us most special of all. What special things has God given us to help us protect and care for ourselves?

Dear Jesus,
Thank You for making me the special person I am. Amen.

Come to Me.
Matthew 11:28

Fix-It Time

The fan broke yesterday at our house. The fan was helping us keep cool. Can you pretend to be a fan?

There are lots of different ways to be a fan. You can blow, just like a fan moves air. Try it. You can wave your arms around. Did you move like the blades of a fan?

A fan motor makes a little noise. Can you whirr? Are you cooling the air around you?

We didn't know how to fix the fan. But somebody came, and she was a great fan fixer. Now the air is moving around in our house, and it feels cooler.

Some people call Jesus a "fix-it person." They tell Him their problems and think He will fix everything right away.

It's good to talk to Jesus about problems. But sometimes Jesus doesn't fix problems the way *we'd* like Him to. Jesus takes care of us in the way that's best for us— whether we know it or not. He solves our problems because He loves us.

Prayer suggestion: Share your problems with Jesus.

God … stopped working.
Genesis 2:2–3

Out for Breakfast

"Get up, get up," Mommy called. "We're going out for breakfast."

"Out for breakfast?" Tabitha thought. What did that mean?

Tabitha came slowly into the kitchen. Mommy was already dressed. Daddy was singing in the bathroom.

"Get dressed, honey," Mommy said. "We're going to eat breakfast at a restaurant."

"Breakfast at a restaurant?" Tabitha asked. "Why?"

"It's the first day of vacation, and we always do fun and different things on vacation," Mommy answered.

Tabitha wasn't sure she wanted to get dressed up and rush to a fancy restaurant. But she took out her clothes and started dressing. When Mommy came into her room, Tabitha thought, vacation time is going to be different this year.

"Where did vacations start?" Tabitha asked. "I mean, whose idea was it?"

"Well," Mommy said slowly. "I guess it was one of God's good ideas. After He created the world, He took a break. We'll look that up in the Bible when we get home from the restaurant."

You can read the story of God's vacation in Genesis 2:2–3.

Dear Jesus,

Thank You for new places to visit, new people to meet, new foods to taste, and for always being with me. Amen.

Those who sleep in death will also be raised.
1 Corinthians 15:20–22

Will You Die?

"I love you, Daddy,"

"Why Travis, what a nice thing to say," said Daddy. "It's not even Valentine's Day or my birthday. I like it when you tell me you love me."

"If I love you enough, Daddy, maybe you won't ever die," said Travis.

"I hope you love me and love me and love me," said Daddy. "But loving me won't keep me from dying. Someday I will die, but I pray that's a long time from now."

"But I don't want you to die—ever!" said Travis.

Do you ever worry about someone dying? Talk about it now with the person who's reading to you.

Dear Jesus,

Sometimes I wonder what would happen if I had to live without my Mommy or Daddy—and I get scared. When I worry about that, help me think instead about how blessed I am to live with them now and with You. Thank You for love—especially Yours. Amen.

Jesus Christ ... is God's "Yes."
2 Corinthians 1:19–20

Amen, Amen

Instructions: Clap each time a star appears above a word.

Do you know what the word *Amen* means?

Amen means "Yes, that's right!" Here is a clapping poem that will help you remember the meaning of *Amen*.

    ★   ★   ★   ★
I know that Jesus is my God.
  ★
Amen!

    ★   ★   ★   ★
And He was born on Christmas—Yes!
   ★
That's right!

    ★   ★   ★ ★
And Jesus is the only One ...
  ★
Amen!

    ★   ★   ★
Who gave His life to save me. Yes!
   ★
That's right!

  ★   ★   ★   ★
I know that Jesus loves me much.
  ★
Amen!

    ★   ★   ★   ★
By name He knows me—calls me. Yes!
  ★
That's right!

Prayer suggestion: Make up your own clapping prayer to Jesus.

I saw the Holy City.
Revelation 21:1–4

Home Sweet Home

Imagine all the different places you could live, then play this word game.

The tallest place to live would be_____.

I'd like to live up there because _____.

The hottest place to live would be _____.

I'd like to live there because_____.

The most fun place to live would be_____.

I'd like to live there because_____.

Someday everyone who knows and loves Jesus will live with Him in heaven. We don't know very much about that place, but it will be better than a tree house, a castle, or a houseboat.

God's people have been hearing about heaven for many years. You can learn what they heard by reading about heaven in the Bible. Even people long ago wanted to go to heaven.

Dear Jesus,

Sometimes I think about heaven. What I don't understand is _____ . I know, though, that You will be in heaven with me. Amen.

163

We are called God's children.
1 John 3:1

Smile Time

What makes you happier—giving a present or getting a present? Why?

What makes you happier—Easter or your birthday? Why?

What makes you happier—getting new shoes or new clothes? Why?

Show how you smile.

There are many times we can be very, very happy. Those times can be wonderful. Sometimes we expect to be happy. Sometimes we just smile right away. Can you smile now? Smile! God loves you!

Prayer suggestion: Talk to Jesus about a time when you were very happy.

*I am writing this to you so that you
may know that you have eternal life.*
1 John 5:11–13

Writing a Book

"Mommy, why do you always sit at the typewriter?" Angela asked.

"Because I have a big job to do," Mommy replied. "I have to write a book."

"We can get books from the library," Angela said.

"You're right," Mommy said, laughing. "But this is a special job for me. Typing this book is one of the most important things I will do in my whole life."

"It doesn't seem so special," Angela said. "You sure throw away a lot of papers."

"That's because I want each page to be very good," Mommy said. "In my book, I want to help children learn about Jesus. That's very important to me."

Jesus is very important to Angela's mother. She wants you to know how much Jesus loves you, that He cares for you, and how special you are as a child of God. That's why Angela's mother sat at the typewriter so much. She wrote this book about Jesus for you.

You can tell other people about Jesus, too. It's exciting work. It's also a very important job.

Dear Jesus,

I can't preach a sermon yet, but I can still tell my friends about You. I can't write a book yet, but I can sing songs about You. I can't build a church yet, but I can bring a friend to church. I can be a good helper, Jesus, right now! Amen.

He spreads snow like a blanket.
Psalm 147:16–17

An Ice Day

It's been summer for several months now. Are you getting tired of the hot weather? Amy is—and she's bored. She wants to play outside, but it's too hot. She's tired of playing inside. What can she do? What do you do when you're bored on hot summer days?

"Amy, don't just sit around the house again today," Mother said. "Do something."

"What?" asked Amy.

"I have an idea," said Mother. "Put on your swimsuit and come into the back yard."

As Amy raced for her suit, she heard her mother take ice cubes from the freezer. What do you think her mother was doing?

In the back yard, Amy's mother dumped lots of ice cubes into the cooler. Then she cut open a big plastic bag and laid it on the grass.

"Why don't you make an ice castle?" Mother suggested. "Use all the cubes you want."

Amy sat in the middle of the plastic, surrounded by the cold, slippery ice. It was hard getting the castle finished before the ice melted, but she had a great time.

At bedtime, Amy prayed:

Thank You, God, for mommies and daddies,
grandmas and grandpas, and everybody else
who has such good ideas. Amen.

Prayer suggestion: Thank Jesus for the people who give you good ideas.

From Paul ... to the church of God.
1 Corinthians 1:1–3

Thinking of You

"Why do you write so many letters to people?" Shannon asked her mother.

"Because I miss them," Mother said. "I like them to know what I'm doing, and I like to hear what my friends are doing, too. I save their letters in a box. Then, when I feel lonely, I reread those letters, and I feel better."

"Nobody ever sends me a letter," Shannon said.

"Not yet," Mother said, "but you do have some real letters—here in the Bible."

"Letters in the Bible?" Shannon asked.

"That's right," Mother said. "Look, here's a letter that a man named Paul wrote to people in a town named Corinth. And here's a letter he sent to his friends in another town."

Ask someone to show you the different sections of the Bible. Can you find letters that people wrote to each other?

The Bible is sort of like God's love letter to us. The Bible isn't just to save, but to read—again and again.

And prayer is sort of like our love letter back to God. Ask the person reading this to help you write your letter to God today.

Dear Jesus,

_____.

_____.

Amen.

Be thankful. . . .
Colossians 3:15–17

Box City

"Grandma, Grandma! Look what Mari's daddy just brought over," N. J. said excitedly. "This is going to be great."

When Grandma looked out the window, all she saw was boxes everywhere.

"Mari's dad is cleaning out the office, and he's letting us have the boxes," N. J. said. "We're making a city."

Outside, Mari said, "I'll make a furniture store. I can bring out pillows for the furniture."

"I'll make a restaurant," another friend said. "We'll serve all kinds of cereal."

Every child had an idea, except N. J. What else did a city need? Then he thought of something. "I'll make the church," N. J. said. "It will be the happiest place in town."

What do you think N. J. will do to make his box look like a church? Is your church one of the happiest places in your town?

Dear Jesus,

Thank You for giving me a place to live, places to shop, and a place to come and sing songs about You. I like to go to church because _____ . Amen.

*I am going to cause food to rain down
from the sky.*
Exodus 16:4

A Liquid Lunch

"What do you want for lunch, Jake?" Dad asked.

"It's too hot to eat," Jake answered. Fan yourself to keep cool like Jake did.

"It is hot," Dad said. "But our bodies need lots of liquids these days. Let's just drink some lunch."

"Drink lunch?" Jake wasn't sure he had heard correctly.

"Sure," Dad said. "Let's go to the garden and pick a nice green pepper and a couple tomatoes."

Back inside, Jake's dad washed the vegetables. Pretend you are washing the green pepper.

"Aw, you're just fixing a salad," Jake said.

"I was teasing a little," Dad said, "but we will be eating lots of liquids. Lettuce is made mostly of water. Carrots, too, are filled with watery juice." How would you pull a carrot out of the ground?

"Carrots don't feel juicy," Jake said. "They're chompy."

"Carrots are hard because they're built out of a bunch of little boxes called cells. The cell walls are crunchy fibers that hold the carrot together," Dad explained. "Each little box is filled with juicy liquid."

"I'm getting hungry," said Jake. "Let's thank God for this liquid lunch—and then let's eat!"

What foods have helped you keep cool this summer?

Dear Jesus,

Thank You for foods and drinks that help cool us this summer. I really like _____ . Amen.

We will tell the next generation
about the Lord's power and His great deeds.
Psalm 78:1–4

A Bible Bookworm

"Girls, you aren't well enough to get out of bed yet," Mother said. "I want you to stay quiet again today. But you are well enough to make a Bible bookworm."

"A Bible bookworm?" they asked together. "What's that?"

"I'll make you a long blank bookworm out of paper," Mother explained. "You take turns telling each other Bible stories. For every story you finish, color one section of the bookworm."

The girls settled down on the couch and started telling Bible stories. The first one was about Noah's ark. What color should they color the bookworm?

Then they told about Queen Esther. What color should they color the bookworm?

Now the girls told about Jesus calming the storm. What color should they use now?

Now you tell a Bible story. Maybe you can start your own Bible bookworm.

Dear Jesus,
Thank You for giving us the Bible. Amen.

May the Lord ... give you peace.
2 Thessalonians 3:16

The Shivers!

Grey was sitting in a wet swimming suit. He started to shake a bit. Grey had the shivers. Shiver with Grey.

Nicholas felt the wind turn cool. He was chilly. Nicholas had the shivers. Shiver with Nicholas.

Megan heard a scary story. She had the shivers. Shiver with Megan.

What gives you the shivers? Different things cause different people to get the shivers. Different things make different people happy. People get sad for lots of reasons.

But knowing that Jesus cares for us can make us all smile. Knowing that Jesus will have a place for us in heaven can make each of us feel warm and cozy inside. And that's a really nice feeling, isn't it?

Dear Jesus,
Thank You for being my Savior. Amen.

Give thanks to the Lord!
Isaiah 12:2–6

Good Smells

Instructions: Every time you hear the word "smell," sniff or use your nose to smell.

Vacation was over. Katherine's family was heading home. She closed her eyes and leaned back in the car.

"Remember how good breakfast *smelled* this morning?" Katherine asked.

"My nose was cold," her brother said. "Breakfast *smelled* warm."

"There's nothing as good as the *smell* of coffee on the last morning of a campout," Mom said.

"Oh, yes, there is," Katherine answered. "I loved our trip. But I can't wait to *smell* our house."

"*Smell* the house?" her brother laughed. "That's funny!"

"But every place has a certain *smell*," Katherine said.

"Grandma's house *smells* like her powder," Dad said.

"I love the way Aunt Gertrude's house *smells* at Thanksgiving," said Katherine. "I can almost taste the turkey by remembering the *smell*."

"I like the *smell* of church at Christmas," Mom said. "Church always *smells* of love and friends; but at Christmas it just seems extra special."

Katherine sat quietly, waiting to *smell* her house. Next Sunday, she would use her nose at church.

Does your church smell of love and friends? Use your nose next time you are there.

Dear Jesus,
Thanks for my wonderful nose. Amen.

God first loved us.
1 John 4:19–21

Mirror, Mirror

Pretend that you have a mirror in front of you. Hold up your hand, with your fingers together, in front of your face. Don't bump your nose!

Now look into your pretend mirror. What can you see? Are your cheeks suntanned? What color are your eyes? What else can you "see"?

Now can you see answers to these questions by looking in your mirror? What's your name? Are you friendly when you play with others? What's your favorite thing to do in the summer?

Now put your mirror down.

We can learn some things by looking in a mirror. There are other things we cannot learn by seeing a reflection.

One thing that does not show up in a mirror is the love of God that is all around us. Although He fills us up with love, we cannot see that in a mirror. But our friends can see what His love does for us. They can see that love when we share. Other people can see God's love when we say nice things. Maybe someone else will see God's love in us when we are forgiving.

Now hold up your mirror again and smile!

I can see how you feel about God's love.

Prayer suggestion: Tell God how you feel now.

You are to go to those lost sheep.
Matthew 10:2–10

A Busy Dozen

Ask someone to help you count up to a dozen. Did you count up to 12?

That's how many helpers Jesus had when He worked here on earth. If you had been one of those busy dozen people, what would you have done? You can read in the Bible what Jesus' helpers did.

You and I weren't one of the first 12 helpers, but we can still tell people about Jesus.

Now count as high as you can in just one minute. What a good helper you could be for Jesus if you could tell that many people about Him!

Prayer suggestion: Tell Jesus how you feel about being one of His helpers.

Believe in the Lord Jesus.
Acts 16:22–34

Let's Pretend

"Let's pretend," Kelessie said to Daniel. "I'm going to be a carpenter." What do you think Kelessie did with her hands?

"I'm going to be a baker," said Daniel. Do something a baker might do.

"Now guess what I am," Kelessie said. She spread her arms wide and carefully walked with one foot behind another. What do you think Kelessie was acting out?

"Guess who I am now," Daniel said. He started to sing "Jesus Loves Me." (Whom was Daniel acting like?)

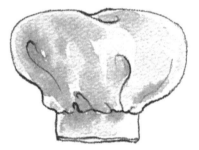

Dear Jesus,

It will be a while before I get a job, but I like to think about what work I might do. I know that I can already do one job for You: Tell my friends about You. Amen.

Ask, and you will receive.
Matthew 7:7–8

Who Ever Listens to Me?

"Dad?" Bethany asked.

"Uh-huh," he answered.

"Can you read a book to me now?" Bethany asked

"Uh-huh," he answered.

"Here's the book," said Bethany.

"Uh-huh," he answered.

"Dad, are you listening?" Bethany asked. "Don't you ever listen to me?"

"Uh-huh," he answered. Dad continued to read the newspaper.

Has something like this ever happened to you?

Sometimes people don't listen to each other. But there's someone who will always make time for you. That's Jesus. He wants to know what you feel, how you are doing, and what's important to you.

Jesus never says, "Uh-huh." Jesus always says, "I promise to listen to you. I promise to love you."

Prayer suggestion: Talk to Jesus now.

Wipe away my sins!
Psalm 51:1–2

Miss Jelly Face

"Angela, how did you get the jelly jar down from the shelf?" asked Mother.

Angela just stared at her. She didn't have anything in her hands. There wasn't even anything in her mouth. How could her mother know she had disobeyed and reached for the jelly jar? What do you think?

"Come here, Miss Jelly Face," said Mother. "We've got to get you cleaned up."

Angela ran off crying. "You don't love me," Angela sobbed. "You're yelling at me."

That evening, when Angela's mother came to kiss her for bedtime, her mother prayed, "Jesus, I'm sorry I got so angry. Please help me be more patient with Angela."

What was Angela's prayer?

Prayer suggestion: Ask Jesus to help your family always be forgiving.

*Everything is to be received
with a prayer of thanks.*
1 Timothy 4:4–5

What's in a Lunch Box?

Trent set his brand-new lunch box on the kitchen counter. Packing a new lunch box was one of the best parts of starting back to school.

First he picked up something in a plastic bag. It wasn't from the refrigerator. What do you think he packed?

Next he took some things from the refrigerator. He packed one item quickly before it rolled off the counter. What did he pack?

Then he packed something wrapped in plastic. It looked delicious. What do you think it was?

Last of all, he poured something into his thermos. What would you like to drink for lunch?

Trent looked at all the things he had packed. Sandwich, fruit, a treat, and something to drink. "Everything's there," he thought.

Then he looked at the lid. His mother had taped a note there. She had written a new lunchtime prayer for him. That would be nice today!

A new school year, a new lunch box, even a new lunch prayer. Trent was ready for a new day.

Do you say a different prayer at each meal or do you use the same prayer?

Prayer suggestion: Trade mealtime prayers with friends so you can learn lots of new ways to say, "Thank You, Jesus, for my food and for the people who grow it and fix it."

Let us go to the Lord's house.
Psalm 122:1

Sunday Best

Evan watched as his dad rubbed and rubbed. Dad put a little more polish on the shoe, and then he rubbed some more. He turned the shoe over and then rubbed it all over with a clean cloth. What was Evan's dad doing?

"Why do you polish your shoes on Saturday nights?" Evan asked.

"When I was a little boy, we always tried to look our best for Sunday morning," Dad explained. "My folks said we should dress up to go into God's house."

"Is that why I wear Sunday pants to church?" Evan asked.

"That's right," said Dad. "Some of the things I learned about church when I was a little boy I'm teaching you now.

"What else am I teaching you about church?" Dad asked. "You might have to think a bit because you might not even know you're learning."

"Well, I know church is where you learn about Jesus," Evan said. "And I know we always like to go to church."

What are *you* learning about church? about Jesus? Will you someday tell those things to your children, too?

Dear Jesus,
You are important to me. I'm glad teachers and others help me learn more about You. Amen.

Love one another.
John 15:12–13

A Letter for You

Let's pretend the mail has just come. You go to your mailbox. How do you open it? Look, there's a letter addressed to you. How does your face look when you see it?

Now pretend to open your letter. It's postmarked "Heaven." Who might have written to you? The letter is signed "Jesus."

If Jesus wrote you a letter, what would He say? Jesus could say many things to you. I don't know exactly what He would say to *you,* but I know it would be signed "Love, Jesus." That's because He loves you. That's the most important message you'll ever get.

If you wrote Jesus a letter, what would you say? I know you would end it with "Love, (*your name*)."

Dear Jesus,
    You love me. I know that. You also love my friends: _____ and _____. You also love my family: _____ and _____ and _____. You love the people who live right next door: _____ and _____.
Thank You, Jesus. Amen.

We are witnesses of everything.
Acts 10:37–43

It's Fall!

"Look, look," Mary said with excitement. "The first colored leaf. It's fall. It's fall! It's really fall!"

Fall leaves are so beautiful. What color leaf do you think Mary found? What color leaves have you found? Colored leaves are a sign that a new season is coming. Summer will soon be over. We can see that now.

We can touch the leaves. We can crunch them. We can smell the autumn leaves burning. That's real proof that fall is coming.

Some people like proof for everything. Some people even want proof that Jesus is around. But we can't reach out and touch Jesus. We can't give Him a hug. We can't say what clothes Jesus is wearing today.

But we know about Jesus. We can read about Him in the Bible. We know Jesus cares about us. He gives us people who love us, who will pray with us.

Jesus' death on the cross for us was proof of His love for us. Easter was many months ago. But the meaning of Easter—that Jesus rose from death—is the same at any time of year.

Jesus loves us. Jesus died for us. We know that, for sure.

Prayer suggestion: Say a special fall prayer.

We saw His star.
Matthew 2:1–2, 9–11

Pick a Little Bit o' Christmas

"It's apple-picking time. It's apple-picking time," Elizabeth sang merrily as she danced around the house.

"Everybody ready?" Grandpa called. "Time to pick a little bit o' Christmas."

"I thought we were going apple picking," Elizabeth said. "What do apples have to do with Christmas?"

"I'll tell you when we get there," Grandpa said.

What a glorious early fall day. Elizabeth picked so many apples that she could hardly carry her bag.

Then Grandpa pulled out a pocket knife and cut a ripe apple across the center. "Look at the center, Elizabeth," Grandpa said.

Elizabeth looked carefully. She had never seen an apple cut across the middle. There was a star right in the center.

"When you pick an apple, you pick a bit o' Christmas," Grandpa explained. "Fresh apples are the first reminder that Christmas is coming."

"And some of these apples are for Christmas dessert," Grandpa added. "We'll put some in the basement until it's time to make the apple pie for Christmas day. We did that when I was a little boy, and now we do the same thing when you're a little girl."

Cut an apple across the center like Elizabeth's grandpa did. Do you see a reminder of the star of Bethlehem?

Dear Jesus,

Thank You for the Christmas reminder hidden in apples. Such a surprise! But I know Your love isn't a surprise. Thank You. Amen.

My help will come from the Lord.
Psalm 121:1–2

A Sad September?

The sun was shining. The weather was warm. The children in the backyard were all having a wonderful time. All except Justin.

Justin was not happy. Justin always got sad around this time of year. Why do you think Justin was unhappy?

September meant there would be changes. There would be fewer days like this to play outside. He would be inside the school building. He wouldn't even get to see some of his favorite friends because they went to a different school.

Justin felt like cutting off the rest of the calendar hanging on the kitchen wall. That way, time would just stop with today. Would that work? What would you say to cheer up Justin?

Dear Jesus,

On good days, I don't want the clock to move. On bad days, time seems to go so slowly. But whatever kind of day it is, I know You are with me. I want to thank You for one special thing that happened recently: _____.
I know You love me, Jesus. Amen.

You were eternally God, and will be God forever.
Psalm 90:1–2

Long Ago

"Did you have a good birthday?" Christopher asked his grandma.

"Oh, yes, it was wonderful," Grandma said. "But now it's time for you to go to sleep."

"Grandma, tell me what it was like when you were a little girl," Christopher said.

"Well, Christopher, we didn't have televisions or computers when I was growing up," Grandma replied.

"How did you live?" Christopher asked.

"Oh, we managed very well," answered Grandma, laughing. "We read lots of books instead of watching TV. And I worked math problems on paper instead of with a calculator."

"Wow," said Christopher. "That's really different."

"Something was the same, though," Grandma said. "We prayed to the same Jesus you pray to every night. We folded our hands just like you do. And we thanked God for all His blessings."

Ask an older person what it was like when he or she grew up. What kind of clothes did people wear to church? What kind of songs did people sing? Can you pretend to have an old-fashioned church service?

Dear Jesus,

Thank You for being there to help people I love when they were little. Thank You for watching over me now. Amen.

The rainbow appears.
Genesis 9:12–17

Happy Rainbow Day!

Kent looked out the window. He couldn't wait for the rain to stop. Little drops still came down, so he couldn't go out to play, yet.

Then he sat up quickly. Something else was happening!

"Aunt Ina, come quick," Kent called. A pale band of colors appeared in the sky.

"That's neat, Kent," Aunt Ina said. The colors were so faded that the rainbow was hard to see. They both watched for a few minutes.

"It's gone," Kent said sadly. "And now it's raining even harder."

"That's all right," Aunt Ina said. "Why don't you make a rainbow inside. That might cheer you up."

"I don't know how," Kent said sadly.

Aunt Ina looked around the room. She began collecting little cars and trucks. First she lined up all the red vehicles, then the orange, then yellow.

"Oh, what fun!" said Kent as his aunt finished the toy rainbow. Kent also cut up old magazines and made rainbows from the colored pictures. When the rain stopped, he made rainbows on the sidewalk with colorful chalk.

How can you have a rainbow day?

Dear God,

Thank You for sending the first rainbow to Noah. When I see a rainbow, I think of Your promise to take care of me. Amen.

His love is eternal.
Psalm 136:1

Cooking Time

Claire was going to help her mother cook supper. It was her very first time at really helping.

"Claire, cooking is very exciting," Mother said. "Tonight you'll see some of our foods get bigger after cooking, and some get smaller."

That's funny, Claire thought. She washed her hands and took some ground meat. She copied her mother as she made a hamburger patty. Would that get bigger or smaller after it was cooked?

Next Claire washed some spinach leaves. She stuffed them into a very large pot but the lid hardly fit. If that got bigger after cooking, it would go all over the kitchen, Claire thought. What happens to spinach while it cooks?

"Turn on the oven light, Claire," Mother said. "How is the bread doing?"

"It's growing," Claire said.

"And so are you," Mother said as she hugged her. "You are a real help in the kitchen. On days like this, I am so grateful God gave you to me to be my daughter. Jesus and I will always love you, honey. I want you to remember that."

You, too, are growing up. You are able to do new things. But no matter how much you grow or change, Jesus will always love you, too.

Dear Jesus,

I never get tired of hearing that people love me. I know You love me, too. Amen.

My heart praises the Lord.
Luke 1:46–55

A Singin' Saturday

"Get the rake, Mindy Sue," Dad called. "We've got lots of leaves over here."

Mindy Sue started raking. But, oh, did she frown.

"Mindy Sue, hold this ladder while I clean out the gutter," Mom said.

Mindy Sue steadied the ladder. But, oh, did she frown.

"Mindy Sue, clean out this toy box in the garage," Dad said.

Now Mindy Sue was really frowning. But then Mindy Sue stopped frowning.

Mom brought out a tape recorder. The first song was "Silent Night." The whole family, except Mindy Sue, started singing. Can you sing "Silent Night"?

The next song was "Angels We Have Heard on High." When the family started singing the long "Gloria," Mindy Sue finally smiled. Do you remember how the "Gloria" goes?

Sing with Mindy Sue—and smile just like Mindy Sue. It doesn't have to be Christmas to remember the birth of Jesus.

Prayer suggestion: Sing another of your favorite Christmas songs for your prayer to Jesus.

Your sins are forgiven for the sake of Christ.
1 John 2:12

I Forgive You

Lissa looked sadly at her sweater. The brand-new school sweater didn't look new anymore. Next time she'd try to remember to bring it in from the playground. But now she was worried. What would her mother say? What do you think might happen?

"Mommy," Lissa called, "I'm home."

"How was school, honey?"

"Fine," Lissa said. "Something happened to my sweater."

"Your new sweater?" Mother said. "What could have happened? It's not even raining or muddy outside."

Lissa held it up. The sweater had dirty footprints all over it, and it was very wrinkled. What had happened to it?

"Well, at least you brought it home," Mother said. "Accidents happen. I'll scrub it right away. Please get the soap. You can help."

"Sure," Lissa said with relief.

How do you think Lissa felt when Lissa's mother forgave her for damaging the new sweater?

The relief and happiness Lissa felt at not being punished is just a little bit like how we feel with Jesus' forgiveness. He will always forgive us no matter what kind of mistakes we make. Jesus will always have His arms open to us with the message, "Come here, tell Me what happened; of course, I forgive you."

Dear Jesus,

Thank You for forgiving me when I do things that aren't right. Help me learn to forgive others. Amen.

I will bless the person who puts his trust in Me.
Jeremiah 17:7–8

A Leaf Hunt

It's fall. It's fall! Soon the weather will be changing. A new season is coming.

Can you go on a leaf hunt? Soon leaves will be covering the ground in some areas. Are there leaves around your house? Where do you think leaves might be hiding? under a bush? blown against the corner with the garbage cans?

How many fall leaves can you find?

Some people say that God paints the world in color during fall. What are your favorite fall colors?

Dear Jesus,

I think Your world is colorful in all seasons. In spring, the grass is yellow-green. In summer, the sky is blue. Now that it's nearing fall, I see more colors. They are _____
_____ . In winter, the color I see most is
_____ . Thanks, Jesus, for Your colorful world. Amen.

All of God's people send you their greetings.
2 Corinthians 13:11–14

Hello and Good-bye

Alicia looked back sadly at the farm. She wouldn't be back to visit the animals until next spring.

She listened to the "cluck, cluck, cluck." What animal was Alicia hearing?

She looked back toward the animal that had been so cute and cuddly last spring. Now it was almost grown up. What animal did she see?

Alicia was going to miss the big horse most of all. Today she had picked a fresh, ripe apple from the tree. The horse had taken it right from her hand! Now the big animal stood by the fence, swishing its tail.

"Look, Alicia, the horse you like is waving good-bye with its tail," Father said.

Alicia sat glumly in the car. All the way home, she remembered the wonderful summer times at the farm.

When they got home, Alicia walked slowly into the house. There was her cat, Princess, waving her tail.

"Well, look at that," Father said, "Princess is saying hello with her tail."

"I like hellos better than good-byes," Alicia said. "Good-bye is such a sad thing."

"It's not sad when you're waving to me and you're off to the zoo," said Father. "Now, let's get supper."

When is a good-bye happy for you?

Dear Jesus,

Some good-byes really make me feel sad. When I feel like that, help me remember I can talk to You. Amen.

The wind blows ... but you do not know where it comes from or where it is going.
John 3:5–8

Jesus Is Near

Here's a wind game to play.

Blow in. Blow out. Now lick your finger. Now blow it. Can you feel the wind you made? Sometimes it takes a wet finger to feel the wind. Moving air is all around us, even if we can't always feel it.

In some ways, Jesus is like the wind. He is always around us, even though we can't see Him. You can make a "Jesus wind strip." Cut pieces of yarn. Tie them on a hanger. Hang your wind strip where you can see it at night.

If you're ever scared at bedtime, or if you can't go to sleep, blow the air around the wind strip. That can remind you that Jesus is always with you.

You are never alone, not even when you sleep. Jesus is with you, always.

Prayer suggestion: Say your favorite prayer to Jesus.

A worm attacked the plant.
Jonah 4:5–7

The Wiggly, Squiggly Ones

"It's only drizzling now," Brian's mother said. "Go out and play under an umbrella."

"Yuck, Mommy," said Brian. "There are wiggly, squiggly worms all over the sidewalk."

"Oh, Brian," Mother said. "Let's go outside and look."

What did Brian and his mother put on to go out in the drizzle?

"It even smells like worms," Brian said once they got outdoors.

"Brian, a worm is an amazing little animal," Mother said. "Look what this worm is doing now." What do you think the worm did?

"Maybe he'll climb up on this stick," Mother said.

"Be careful you don't break his bones," Brian said.

"A worm doesn't have any bones, Brian," Mother said. "No bones, no eyes, and no ears to hear, either."

"I told you worms were yucky," Brian said.

"I think they're amazing," Mother said. "Most of all, worms are God's creatures."

What are some other animals that go outside in the rain?

Dear Jesus,

I never knew much about worms. There's even a worm story in the Bible. I love learning about the animals You created. Amen.

I … give you the harvest season each year.
Jeremiah 5:24

The Smell of September

Julie could smell it was fall. What do you smell in fall? Just yesterday at Julie's house, the air smelled damp. Can you guess what the weather was like? Today, Julie smells smoke. What do you think could be burning?

Julie can also touch fall. When she walks down the sidewalk, something crunches under her feet. What do you think she's crunching?

Julie loves the smell and touch of fall. What are you doing at your house this fall?

Dear Jesus,

Thank You for the different times of year. The thing I like best about fall is _____.
Amen.

I will lead My blind people.
Isaiah 42:16

A Look through Julie's Eyes

Do you remember Julie? Yesterday we talked about fall at her house. We talked about things that you and Julie feel and smell in fall.

Now use your eyes. Look out a window. How can you tell it's fall? Just use your eyes.

Julie can't see the same signs of fall. She is blind. Spring, summer, fall, and winter all look the same to Julie. She can only see a few shadows through her eyes.

Julie uses her ears, her nose, and her hands to learn about things like fall. She learned about Jesus that way, too.

Julie has a friend who tells her stories from the Bible. Julie listens to the words at church. And you should hear Julie sing about Jesus!

Julie can't look at a church and know that it is a place to learn about Jesus. Julie can't see the pretty windows at church that make the sunlight look so colorful.

But Julie knows Jesus loves her. Julie knows Jesus will take care of her in spring, summer, fall, and winter. Julie feels so good about that! How do you feel hearing about Julie and Jesus?

Dear Jesus,
Thank You for my wonderful body. Amen.

To Jesus Christ be the glory and power forever.
Revelation 1:4–6

abc

A Good Question

"Did Jesus ever eat apple pie?" Jared asked his dad.

"That's a good question," Dad said. "Go ask your mom."

"Did Jesus ever eat apple pie?" Jared asked his mom.

"That's a good question," Mom said. "Go ask your grandfather."

"Did Jesus ever eat apple pie?" Jared asked his grandfather.

"That's a good question," Grandfather said. "Go ask ..."

"No, Grandfather," Jared interrupted. "I can't go ask somebody else. I'll just have to ask Jesus when I get to heaven."

What will you want to ask Jesus when you get to heaven?

Prayer suggestion: Tell Jesus what you will ask Him when you get to heaven.

I love the house where You live, O Lord.
Psalm 26:8

A Church Box

"But Mommy, I want to go to church," Sabrina wailed.

"I'm glad you like church," Mommy said, "but you are just not quite ready to go out yet. You need one more day inside, just to be sure that your cold is gone."

"I have to go to church," Sabrina insisted. "It's just not Sunday without church."

"I'm sorry, Sabrina," Mommy said firmly. "You can go next week but not today."

Sabrina sat sadly and looked out the window. It didn't seem like Sunday. She wouldn't hear the pretty music. She couldn't visit with her friends. She couldn't hear about Jesus. Then Sabrina had an idea.

"Mommy, do you have an extra box?" Sabrina asked. "It needs to be pretty big."

"There's an empty box in the front closet that you may have," Mommy answered. "Why do you need it?"

"You'll see," Sabrina said. What do you think Sabrina will do with the box? Sabrina was busy for a long time. She used scissors, crayons, and paper.

When her mother peeked around the door, she saw Sabrina had made the box into a church! Her dolls were all sitting nicely, listening to Sabrina talk about Jesus. Can you make a church box, too?

Dear Jesus,
　　Thank You for giving us our church. I especially like
＿＿＿＿＿＿＿＿＿＿＿＿＿＿＿＿ . Amen.

You ... will be God forever.
Psalm 90:1–2

Changes, Changes

It was fall where Angela lived. The leaves were turning different colors. The temperature was changing, too. The thermometer on the back porch showed it was getting cooler. What kind of clothes would Angela wear to play outside?

Angela's grandpa emptied the swimming pool. Angela put away the sprinkling can and hose.

New seasons bring many changes. But Jesus stays the same in spring, summer, fall, and winter. We can always talk to Jesus. Jesus loves us all year.

Today we start a new month. Fall is a new season. But Jesus is still your best Friend.

Dear Jesus,

It's fall where I live. I like this season because _____
_____. Thank You for giving us a new season. Thank You for staying the same. Amen.

Love one another.
1 John 4:7

Love, Love, Love

"I love you very, very ... " Christina told Aunt Ruth. Christina was trying to tell Aunt Ruth how much she loved her.

Who are people you love? Show one person, right now, that you love him or her.

Did you show love by smiling? When you were a baby, that was the first way you showed love.

Did you show love with a hug or kiss? It feels good to be close to somebody.

Did you tell someone you loved him or her? It's nice to hear, "I love you."

That's what Jesus says when He gives us people who help us grow. Jesus says that, too, when He gives us people who can love us.

Jesus loves each of us "very, very ... " Oops, I forgot a word. Fill it in for me: Jesus loves me very, very _____ .

Dear Jesus,

Thank You for loving me. I love You, too. And thank You for giving me people who help me grow and who love me. Their names are _____ . I love them, too. Amen.

This child is chosen by God.
Luke 2:25–35

Move Over, Baby

We have a baby at our house. His name is Matthew. Today Matthew is five months old. How old are you?

Matthew learned to smile a few months ago. How do you smile? Last month, he learned to put his hands together. Can you hold your hands together? Now Matthew is rolling over. How do you roll over?

Soon Matthew will learn to crawl. You are probably good at crawling. Crawl a little bit, the way you did when you were a baby. Now crawl back to this book.

Soon, too, Matthew will learn about Jesus. What should we tell Matthew about Jesus?

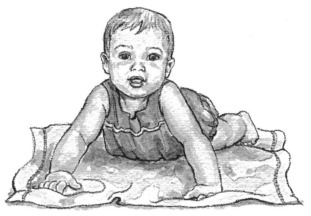

Dear Jesus,

When I was a baby, I didn't know about You. But You loved me anyway. When I was little, I couldn't walk or talk or even smile. Now I can do many things. I can _____ _____ . Also, I now know that You love me and _____ . Amen.

*Even the hairs of your head
have all been counted.*
Matthew 10:29–31

Who Knows It All?

Instructions: Help your child use his or her fingers to show these answers.

How many noses do you have?

How many ears do you have?

How many fingers do you have?

How many hairs do you have on your head?

That last question is hard to answer. Not even grown-ups can tell how many hairs are on their head. But God knows. God knows all about you. God knows you have one nose, two ears, and 10 fingers. In the Bible, Jesus says that God even knows how many hairs are on your head.

God also knows He loves you.

What do you know about God? There are lots of things we might know about God, but one thing is most important: He loves us.

Dear God,

Thank You for knowing all about me—for knowing that I live in _____ , for knowing that I like to play with _____ , for knowing that my name is _____ , and for loving me. I _____ You, too. Amen.

I pray to You all day long.
Psalm 86:3–5

Don't Forget

It was almost bedtime. Brett's mom helped him take off his play clothes. He wiggled into his pajamas. Brett went to the bathroom and then brushed his teeth. It was time for listening to a book. Then the night light blinked on.

"Good night, Brett. I love you," said Mom as she tucked the covers around him.

"But Mommy, you forgot something," said Brett. What did his mother forget?

Talking to Jesus, or praying, is something to do every day. Brett and his mom always pray together before going to sleep at night. Some people pray before eating a meal. Some people pray when they wake up in the morning. When do you pray?

Jesus doesn't count how often you pray. He doesn't keep track of when you pray. He just wants to hear from you.

Prayer suggestion: Tell Jesus about your day.

You will be witnesses for Me.
Acts 1:8

Witness

Let's do some pretending with sounds.

What would one day say to another day?

How would an alligator talk to a crocodile?

What kind of sound would a daddy lion make to a mommy lion?

What would you say to a friend about Jesus?

When you tell somebody about Jesus, you are being a witness. *Witness* is a big word. *Witness* is an important word. Telling people about how much Jesus loves them is one of the things we are supposed to do.

You can be a witness. You can tell somebody about Jesus.

Dear Jesus,

I didn't know I could be a witness. That's a big word. Mostly I just want to tell people about You. I know one person I can tell about You. I can tell _____ _____ . Amen.

Jesus wept.
John 11:32–36

About Dying

Scott was angry. His grandpa had died. Now Grandpa can't take me fishing next summer, thought Scott.

How would you feel if someone died?

Some people feel guilty (even though they aren't). How do you know when someone feels guilty?

Some people get sad. How do you know when someone is sad?

Some people get lonesome. What do you do when you're lonesome?

We can tell Jesus how we feel. He wants to know when we hurt inside.

Do you know someone who died? Are you worried about someone dying? Tell the person who is reading this book with you and tell Jesus.

Prayer suggestion: Talk to Jesus about dying.

Let us go to the Lord's house.
Psalm 122:1

Where Am I?

Instructions: Help your child solve these riddles about buildings.

I am a place where you buy things.
You buy food here.
I am a _____.

I am a place you visit when you are sick.
You come here when you don't feel well.
I am a _____.

I am a place where you get money.
You can drive to me, walk to me, or come inside me.
I am a _____.

I am a place where you learn about Jesus.
You see your friends when you come here.
I am a _____.

There are lots of things inside a church. You might sit on a pew or chair. You might hear beautiful music. You might look through pretty glass windows.

But the best thing about church isn't the building. Can you guess what is best? You come to hear about Jesus. That's what's most important about a church.

Dear Jesus,
I'm glad there is a place I can go to learn more about You. Amen.

Join with us in the fellowship.
1 John 1:3

Circles

Make a circle with your fingers. Make a circle with your arms.

Now ask someone to make a circle around you. Who is in the center of the circle? When you're in the center of a circle, you feel really important.

Find a picture of Jesus. Make a circle around the picture with your fingers. You have put Jesus in the center of your circle. He is an important part of that circle.

Because you are a child of God, Jesus wants to be at the center of your life. That means that when you play, He wants you to act as His child. When someone asks for help, He wants you to act as He would. He wants to be important in your life.

We can't go around holding our fingers in a circle to remember that Jesus is at the center of our lives, but we can try to do things like a child of God.

Dear Jesus,

I try to remember to act like Your child. I am kind to people in my family and to my friends. I try to share. I also
_____. Amen.

While we were still sinners … Christ died for us!
Romans 5:8

It's Not Fair

"It's just not fair," Emily told her mommy. "Kristin gets to go to a party and I don't."

"It's just not fair," Tom told his dad. "David is going on vacation. We never go anywhere."

"It's just not fair," Megan said to Muneeza. "Teacher always sends Mark on errands just because he gets done so fast with his schoolwork."

Have you ever said, "It's not fair"? Do you think it's fair that Jesus loves us? We all do wrong. At some time, each of us has acted poorly. There are times we don't do what we should. But Jesus doesn't punish us. He forgives us.

It's just not fair that Jesus loves us even though we do bad things. It's not fair, but it's true. No matter what we do, no matter how we act, Jesus still loves us.

Dear Jesus,
Thanks for everything. Amen.

There is a boy here. ...
John 6:5–13

Not Too Little

"You're too little."

How do you feel when someone says that to you? You are too young to drive a car, to bake a cake all by yourself, or to use the lawn mower.

But you aren't too little for some things. What are some things you are good at doing?

There's another thing you aren't too little for: being God's child. How old are you? That's certainly old enough to be loved by Jesus.

Now, think, whom can you tell about Jesus? What can you say about Jesus?

You're not too little for Jesus. You're just right.

Dear Jesus,

You know how old I am. You know that I am _____ years old. That is old enough to be Your helper. Being Your helper makes me feel _____.
Amen.

The new has come.
2 Corinthians 5:17

Something New

Instructions: After every statement with a ★, ask your child to show with a sad or a happy face how he or she feels.

Albert was so excited. He was going to get new shoes.★ But the first day Albert wore the shoes, they made his feet hurt.★

Nicholas was getting a new Sunday school teacher.★ But Nicholas liked his other teacher.★

Luis was moving to a brand-new house.★ But Luis liked his old house.★

Blake's new baby sister was coming home from the hospital.★ Blake wasn't sure how he felt.★

It might be fun to get something new. It can be exciting or scary, too.

Prayer suggestion: Talk to Jesus about a time when you had something new.

These have been written.
John 20:30–31

Dress-Up

It is almost Halloween. Joe and Lisa are going to dress up like their favorite Bible people this year.

With his costume, Joe needs two cats, two dogs, two birds, and a boat. Whom do you think Joe is dressing like? (Noah)

Lisa is looking for a beautiful crown and colored scarves to tie around her. Whom is Lisa going to dress like? (Queen Esther)

If you could dress up like your favorite Bible person, what would you wear?

Dear Jesus,

It's fun to think about a time long ago when You were a little boy. One of the people I like to hear about in the Bible is _____. Even though I like that person, You will always be the most important person in the Bible. Amen.

A Job for Jesus

Do you know someone who works in an office? who works in a school? who works outdoors?

Many people go to school to learn about their job. They study and practice what they will be doing.

You are learning about your work as you go through the pages of this book. Your job is for Jesus. That's why words about Jesus are on every page. What do you know about Jesus?

Dear Jesus,

I know lots of things about You. I know You love me. I still want to learn this about You: _____.
I can find some answers in Your Book, the Bible. Thanks for giving me the important job of being Your helper. Amen.

Your love ... will always keep me safe.
Psalm 40:11

Just Plain Me

Jennifer and Greg were talking about Halloween. Jennifer was so excited! She was going to wear a clown costume. Greg was not excited. He didn't even want to wear a costume.

"Mommy, I don't want to be a scarecrow," said Greg. "Birds will come and peck me."

"Greg, you will still be yourself on Halloween," said Mom.

"Mommy, I don't want to be a lion either," said Greg. "People will think I bite."

"Greg, you will just be wearing a costume," said Mom. "All that will be different will be your clothes. You'll still be my little boy."

"After Halloween, when I take off the costume, will I be me again?" Greg asked.

"Greg, you'll be you however you dress on Halloween," she said. "You can even dress like my little boy."

Dear Jesus,

Help me remember that You love me just the way I am. You will always love me—no matter what I wear, no matter what I do. You will always love me. Amen.

Each of you must put aside some money.
1 Corinthians 16:2

Money to Give Away

"Money, money, money. I like money," said Courtney as she sat with her teddy-bear bank. "I like to feel the paper money. It's soft. And the coins go clink, clink, clink."

What do you think Courtney will do with her money?

Courtney gave some of her money to God. She couldn't hand it to Jesus, but she took it to church. The church was going to use her money to print a newspaper about Jesus. What other ways could a church use money?

Next time Courtney plays with her teddy-bear bank, she will count out some more money to give to church. Courtney likes to do that. Why do you think giving money to church makes her happy?

Dear Jesus,

Thank You for giving me money that I can save and spend. I know that when I take money to church, I help other people learn about You. Amen.

Rejoice!
Philippians 4:4

Laugh a Lot

Michelle clomped into her daddy's room. "See, I got my shoes and socks on all by myself," she said.

"That's nice, but the shoes are on the wrong feet," Daddy answered.

"Are the socks on the right feet?" Michelle asked.

Why was Michelle's question funny? When did you laugh today? Jesus wants us to be happy and have good times. Tell Jesus about a time you smiled.

Dear Jesus,

I don't always smile. But I want to tell You about a time when I had fun: _____. Amen.

I am the vine, and you are the branches.
John 15:4–7

Lost and Found

John lost a puzzle piece. How do you think John feels?

Tyler can't find the dollar bill he got for Christmas. How do you think Tyler feels?

John found the puzzle piece under his bed. And look— Tyler's money was stuck in a book! What kind of look do these boys have on their faces now?

Every day we feel lots of different ways. Jesus wants to know how we feel. He cares about how we feel. Tell Jesus about your feelings today.

Dear Jesus,
    Today I felt _____ when _____. Sometimes I feel sad when _____. It makes me happy, though, to know that You love me. No matter how I feel, I can always feel good inside because You're smiling at me. That's a warm, friendly feeling, Jesus. Amen.

Hide me in the shadow of Your wings.
Psalm 17:8

No Witches! No Ghosts!

It's the day before Halloween at Benjamin's house. But Benjamin doesn't have a smile on his face.

"Ben, what's the matter?" asked Mom.

"Nothing," said Ben.

"Benjamin, something must be bothering you," she said.

"Nothing's wrong. But don't look up in the sky tomorrow, Mommy," said Ben.

"Why, Ben?" asked Mom.

"You might see a ghost or goblin," said Ben. "I'm not going to look up because a witch might be flying around on a broom. Jerry and Ted said so."

"The boys were just teasing," said Mom. "You know there are no real witches or ghosts or goblins."

"Really?" said Ben. "Oh, wow! I can't wait until tomorrow. It's Halloween!"

Dear Jesus,

I get scared sometimes. Sometimes I'm afraid of _____ _____. Please help me remember, Jesus, that I can always tell You what is scary. I know You'll listen. Amen.

Listen! I stand at the door and knock.
Revelation 3:20–21

Knock, Knock

"Knock, knock." Another trick-or-treater was at the door. It was a busy night at Aretha's house.

"Who are you, really?" Aretha asked the costumed person.

"I'll give you a clue," said the voice behind the mask. "I'm family."

"Oh, Jason, Jason, I know your voice," Aretha said happily as her cousin took off the mask.

If Jesus stood at your door and knocked, He might say much the same thing. "You're family," He might say. You're part of His family. He loves you.

Prayer suggestion: Tell Jesus how you feel about Him.

We have found the Messiah.
John 1:40–42

Shout It Out

Jump like a kangaroo.

Sing like a bird.

Can you wag your tail like a dog?

Have you ever felt like a turtle with its head inside the shell?

Sometimes it feels good to be all alone. Name a time you wanted to hide. Did you ever feel like hiding when somebody asked you about Jesus? I hope not. I hope you wanted to tell that person how much Jesus loves you.

Sing like a bird when you answer this question: "Who is Jesus?"

Roar like a lion to answer this: "Whom does Jesus love?"

Do people understand what you said when you sang like a bird or roared like a lion?

This time, talk like you usually talk and answer this question: "What's important about Jesus?"

Dear Jesus,
  Help me tell other people about You. Amen.

Have your sins washed away.
Acts 22:16

Cleaning Up

What can you wash with a rag and a bucket of water?

What can you clean with some soap and water?

What room in your house needs some cleaning right now?

Churches need cleaning, too. Who cleans your church? Do you know who wipes off the Sunday school chalkboard? Have you ever seen someone wash the church windows?

What's your favorite thing to clean?

Dear Jesus,

Thanks for water. I like to play in it. I like to splash in it. I like to _____ . Water helps us keep things clean, too. Thanks, Jesus, for water. Amen.

In His Word I trust.
Psalm 130:5–6

Extra Thanks

Ryan was so excited! He was getting a new wheelchair. His arms got very tired moving the wheels of his old chair.

Ryan loved to bounce balls on the playground. And when his friends played kickball, Ryan would kick the ball with the side of the chair. But now he was getting a chair that moved with the touch of a switch. And it was coming today!

Ryan hung around the house all day. By suppertime, the delivery truck still hadn't come. Ryan and his mother looked at the order. The date was for next week!

Sunday, Monday, Tuesday—the week was going so slowly! Finally, it was a week later. Ryan was afraid the new chair wouldn't come, so he wheeled off to play.

When he rolled home for lunch, he saw an empty packing crate. Ryan could feel his heart thumping. There, inside the kitchen, was the new wheelchair.

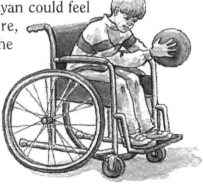

Ryan was so excited that when he finally zoomed to the table for lunch, he added some extra words to the mealtime prayer. What do think Ryan told Jesus?

Dear Jesus,

Sometimes I forget to thank You for little things that are really important. Thanks, Jesus for _____. Amen.

The old things have disappeared.
Revelation 21:3–4

Look Ahead!

"Guess what I'm going to be next Halloween," Kimiko said.

"Why, Kimiko, we just had this Halloween," Grandmother answered.

"I know—but guess what I'm going to be next Halloween," Kimiko repeated.

Are you looking forward to next Halloween, too? It's fun to think ahead. Are you eager for Christmas to come?

We look forward to things we enjoy. We all look forward to being in heaven with Jesus. In heaven, no one will get sick or be afraid. No one will cry. Best of all, we will live with Jesus and be able to see Him.

Prayer suggestion: Talk to Jesus about heaven.

Respect your father and your mother.
Exodus 20:12

Helping Each Other

"Rachel, time to clean up your room," said Daddy.

"But Daddy, it's too much room," answered Rachel.

"It's time to clean it up, Rachel," he said again.

"I'm too tired," said Rachel. "And besides, it's too messy to clean up all by myself."

"I didn't want to stop what I was doing yesterday and drive you to that birthday party," Daddy reminded her, "but we need to help each other."

Who are some people God gives to help you?

Dear Jesus,

Thank You for giving me these people to love me: ____ _____. Thank You for giving me these people to help me grow up: _____. Amen.

Jesus was there alone.
Matthew 14:22–23

Alone Time

"Leave me alone," shouted Aneko.

"What's wrong with you?" her sister asked.

"I just want some alone time," said Aneko. "Let me be by myself."

Being alone is important for everybody. Where do you go to be alone?

When Jesus lived on earth, He liked alone time, too. He would sometimes go away by Himself to rest. Sometimes He would sleep. Sometimes He would pray. What do you do when you're alone?

Dear Jesus,

I'm glad You understand what it is like to want to be alone. Thank You for always being with me, even when I am alone. Amen.

So great is His love for [them].
Psalm 103:11–13

Who Started It?

"He started it!"

"No, she did!"

"He did."

"She did."

Can you tell what's going on here? It's an argument. It's not much fun to argue. It doesn't make me feel good when I disagree with someone.

It's not good to argue. But there is one good thing: Jesus will forgive us. Even if we start a disagreement, Jesus will still forgive us.

Dear Jesus,
   Thank You for always forgiving me. Amen.

He is Jesus.
John 1:45–46

God's House

Let's pretend. Imagine the most wonderful place to live in the whole wide world. Will your imaginary house have elevators? a big zoo in the back yard? toys in every room?

Think of the place where you really live. Is there space for you to sleep? Can you look out a window? Can you sit down to eat? Those things help make a good place for a child to live.

Church is called the house of God. A church might be a place where you feel like being quiet. A church might have a beautiful tall steeple or pretty windows. But a church doesn't need those things.

A church needs people to come and worship. A church needs you to come and learn about Jesus. A church is a place where you can bring a friend who doesn't know about Jesus. That's what makes a good house of God.

Dear Jesus,

Help me remember that You like it when I come to church. Help me think of someone I can bring with me to Your house, my church. Amen.

Go, then, to all peoples everywhere.
Matthew 28:19–20

Calling You!

Jeremy knows it's suppertime when his grandfather calls, "Come and get it."

Jo Ellyn comes for supper when she hears, "Soup's on."

Wanda runs to the kitchen when her stomach growls.

Who calls you for mealtime?

God calls us, too. He doesn't call us when it's time for a hamburger. He calls us for a more important reason. God calls us to be His helpers. God wants each of us to tell other people about Jesus.

God has called you to be His helper. Now, whom can you tell about Jesus?

Dear Jesus,

I know You have asked me to be Your helper. Help me when I tell other people about You. Amen.

Let the children come to Me.
Mark 10:13–16

Rain, Rain, Go Away

"There's nothing to do," sighed Tony as he looked outside. Rain was streaming down the window. The yard looked soggy after days of wet weather.

"Read a book," said Mother.

"I don't know how to read," said Tony.

"Look at the pictures in a book," suggested Mother.

"I'm tired of all my old books," said Tony.

"Make your own book," she said. "Draw pictures about something. I'll help you put it together."

"All I know about is rain. Rain, rain, rain! That's all it ever does," Tony complained.

"Here's a leftover paper from Sunday school," Mother said. "That might give you some ideas. Why don't you make a book about Jesus?"

Can you help Tony? What could he put in his book about Jesus?

Dear Jesus,

Thank You for giving us the Bible so we can learn more about You. Thank You for Sunday schools and teachers. Amen.

The greatest in the Kingdom ...
becomes like this child.
Matthew 18:1–4

Always God's Child

"I want to be your baby again," said Nikki as she crawled onto her mother's lap.

Have you ever wanted to go back to being little? Show something you did when you were a baby.

Sometimes it might seem nice to be a baby again. Being a baby means you get cuddled and held a lot. But it also means you can't do lots of things you can do now. Show one thing you couldn't do as a baby.

Soon you will be doing more and more things. But you will always be a child of God. Now point to the oldest person in the room. Even that person is still a child of God.

Even though we grow up and do lots of wonderful things, we can always be a child of God. Just as a baby is loved, so God will always love us. A baby needs lots of help. God is always ready to help us because we are His children.

We can be grown up with everybody else, but we can still be a child with God.

Dear Jesus,

Thank You for loving me as Your child. I'm not a baby anymore because I can do lots of things, like _____ _____. But I know You will always love me as Your child no matter how old I get. Amen.

Call to Me when trouble comes.
Psalm 50:15

Call for Help

Elizabeth sat quietly. She knew something serious must have happened. Mommy was so quiet. Daddy looked upset. Something wasn't right.

Elizabeth was worried. What could she do? Then she had an idea. Her parents always told her to talk to Jesus when she had a problem. That's what she'd suggest.

"Mommy, why don't you call God on the telephone and tell Him what's wrong?" Elizabeth suggested.

"That's a good idea," Dad said, smiling. "But we don't have to bother with a phone call. Let's just pray."

Elizabeth sat quietly while her parents prayed. Elizabeth knew God would listen to their words.

Dear Jesus,

Sometimes I forget to ask You for help. I get angry and forget that I can talk to You. Help me remember You are closer than a phone call. You're right here with me. Amen.

He loved us.
1 John 4:10

A Lousy Thanksgiving?

"What a crummy day," Akeem said as he walked into the kitchen.

"Why, Akeem, it's Thanksgiving. How can Thanksgiving be crummy?" asked Aunt Helen.

"It's not just crummy," Akeem answered. "It's a yucky, lousy, icky, crummy day." And he wandered off.

Have you ever felt like Akeem? What makes a bad day for you?

Some days go better than others. That's true for everybody. Sometimes around holidays people think everything should be great for everybody. That's a nice thought, but it doesn't always work out that way. How is the Thanksgiving season for you this year?

There's always one thing that is good about every day: Jesus loves us. Jesus loves us in November, on our birthday, and even when we have a yucky, lousy, icky, crummy day.

Jesus doesn't promise us that every day will be super, but He promises to love us all the time.

Prayer suggestion: Thank Jesus for the ways He has loved you today.

Perfect love drives out all fear.
1 John 4:18

Plenty for All

"I want a drumstick," Deron yelled across the table.

"Deron, your cousins asked for the drumsticks first," Mom reminded him. "They are our guests. You'll have to share."

"I don't want to share. There won't be enough for me," cried Deron.

How do you think Deron feels now? Sometimes sharing doesn't seem like much fun.

There's one thing we can share and still have enough for ourselves: Jesus' love. Jesus has enough love for everybody. There's plenty to go around. Jesus will love us, and love us, and love us—and there still is plenty of love for everybody else, too.

Dear Jesus,
  Thank You for loving me all the time. Amen.

Give thanks to the Lord.
Psalm 136:1

Thanksgiving Every Day

Today is a holiday at Kim's house. Today her family is celebrating Thanksgiving. But Kim doesn't feel like she's celebrating. Let's listen as she talks to her aunt.

"Aunt Rose, why don't we get presents today?" Kim asked.

"Because it's Thanksgiving," Aunt Rose responded.

"My birthday is a holiday, and I get presents. We get lots of presents on Christmas. And on Valentine's Day and Halloween we get things, too. Why can't I get a Thanksgiving present?" Kim asked again.

"On Thanksgiving, we remember the presents we get the rest of the year," said Aunt Rose. "We thank God for the nice meals we eat, for the clothes we wear, for the toys we play with every day."

As Kim listened to Aunt Rose, she remembered other things that were presents to her.

Prayer suggestion: What can you thank God for today?

God loved us.
1 John 4:11

Word Games

Instructions: Help your child finish these sentences.

Jesus loves me. Jesus loves _____.

Jesus forgives me. I can forgive _____.

A word that rhymes with boo is the word _____.

Did you finish those word games with "you"?

You is an important word. You are an important person. God loves you. He cares about you. He gives you people to love, too.

Let's try those word games again.

Jesus loves me. Jesus loves _____.

Jesus forgives me. I can forgive _____.

Can you make up a riddle using *you*?

Prayer suggestion: Ask Jesus to help you love and forgive others because He loves and forgives you.

God has blessed us.
Psalm 67

What a Rainbow World!

Look out the window and spot something green. Now find something blue. Where is something black? Can you find something yellow, purple, and orange, too?

If we look outside, we can usually see a whole bunch of colors. Which color is your favorite?

What a colorful world God has made! Think of all the colors on you right now. Ask someone to tell you all the colors they see in your eyes. Look into someone's eyes. How many colors can you find?

Sometimes November seems like a dull month. But see what beautiful colors you've found!

Dear Jesus,
Thank You for all the colors, especially my favorite color, _____. Amen.

God first loved us.
1 John 4:19

No Friends

"Mommy, Mommy," Jaimie sobbed as she came into the house.

"Mommy, Mommy," Jaimie said, "Kate says my hair looks wilted. She won't let me swing in her yard."

Jaimie's mom looked up and smiled. "It does look like you need a shampoo tonight. Is that all that's wrong?" she said.

"Is that all?" Jaimie wailed. "It's terrible … horrible … awful! I won't ever go to her house again. Now who can I play with?"

How do you feel when someone is mean to you? Have you ever been mean to anyone?

Jesus loves you even when others aren't nice. He forgives you even when you aren't nice. Jesus is the best Friend for us all.

Prayer suggestion: Thank Jesus for your friends.

Let us kneel before the Lord, our Maker.
Psalm 95:6

A Brown Day

"I don't like the color outside," said Stephanie as she looked out the window. "Everything looks brown in fall."

Grandpa came over to look, too. The empty tree branches were brown. The grass had turned brown. Even the leaves that blew on the ground had lost their bright fall colors. Stephanie was right—it was a brown world.

"Look, Grandpa, there goes a squirrel across the telephone wire," said Stephanie. "He's carrying something in his mouth." What do you think the squirrel had?

"It looks like it's something to bury until winter comes," said Grandpa. "I'll bet that squirrel will be glad to see that brown, round thing a few months from now. See how the squirrel is digging up those brown leaves? The leaves will be a good blanket for that bit of food. And see the squirrel's nice, thick, brown coat of fur?"

"You're right, Grandpa," Stephanie said. "Brown isn't a rainbow color, but I'm glad God made brown in our back yard."

Dear Jesus,
    Thank You for making our world so colorful. Amen.

When this first census took place,
Quirinius was the governor of Syria.
Luke 2:1–7

When?

"Did Jesus live before the Pilgrims?" Asad asked his dad.

"Oh, yes, a long time before the Pilgrims," Dad answered.

"Did Jesus live before the cowboys?" Asad asked.

"Oh, yes, a long time before the cowboys," Dad answered.

"Well, when was Jesus born?" Asad asked.

"We don't know exactly when He was born," Dad responded, "but we know for sure that Jesus was born."

Christmas will be coming soon. That's when we celebrate Jesus' birthday. Listen to the story of Jesus' birth in Luke 2:1–14.

Dear Jesus,
    Thank You for being born to be my Savior. Amen.

Whoever welcomes this child
in My name, welcomes Me.
Luke 9:46–48

All Kinds of Shoes

Today we're going to play a word game. First, some questions; then, a riddle. Ready?

The weather is cold and snowy where Martina lives. What will she wear on her feet today?

It rained all night where Carlos lives. It's still raining. How will he dress to go outside?

The temperature is very hot and the sun is shining brightly at Edward's house. What will he wear on his feet?

Now, here's the riddle: How are Martina, Carlos, and Edward alike?

Jesus loves them all. Jesus loves children who go barefoot like Edward, who wear rain boots like Carlos, and who wear warm winter boots like Martina. What do you have on your feet now?

Name some children Jesus loves.

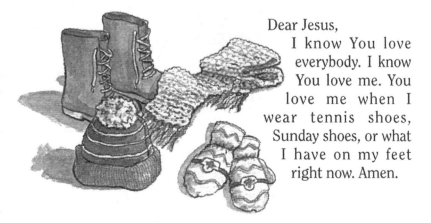

Dear Jesus,
I know You love everybody. I know You love me. You love me when I wear tennis shoes, Sunday shoes, or what I have on my feet right now. Amen.

Mary got ready.
Luke 1:39–45

A Birthday Is to Share

It was almost Donzell's birthday. He was so excited! Donzell and his father were going to shop for party things. What do you think they should buy?

Donzell thought of all the fun he would have at the party. But he was also sad about his party. His best friend couldn't come. Donzell knew the birthday would still be nice. But he was disappointed that his friend wouldn't be there to share the fun.

"Birthdays are better if you share them," Dad said. "That's what is so great about Jesus' birthday. So many people can share Christmas."

Donzell's dad was right. And people are already sharing. We hear Christmas music. The Christmas decorations look so pretty. Jesus' birthday is still a few weeks away, but how are you getting ready?

Dear Jesus,

Your birthday is coming and I'm so _____. Please help me remember the most important thing about Christmas: You were born on the first Christmas. Amen.

I am going to prepare a place for you.
John 14:1–4

Happy in Heaven

When you get into the car, where do you like to go? Do you like to ride to a special place to eat? Is there someone you like to visit?

Someday we will go to the most wonderful place. Someday we will go to heaven. We don't know exactly what heaven will be like, but it will have everything we need to be happy.

Scott hopes he won't have any allergies in heaven. Amanda wants to eat lots of her favorite food in heaven—chocolate ice cream. Mia just wants to be happy.

And we will be happy in heaven. That's what Jesus promises us. What makes you happy? How will your face look when you see Jesus in heaven?

Dear Jesus,

I will be happy to come to heaven. When I see You in heaven, I will want to tell You all about _____. Amen.

The Protector ... never dozes or sleeps.
Psalm 121:2–4

Good Night

It was time to stop playing. Time to put on pajamas. Time to brush teeth. Time to read a book. Time to lie down. What time was it?

Is bedtime a good time for you? Sometimes it feels nice to settle down after a busy day. Sometimes children don't like to clean up toys and stop the fun. You can feel different ways about going to bed on different days.

God made nighttime so we could all sleep. Our bodies get tired, and we need to rest. What are some sounds you hear at bedtime? Do you feel someone kiss you good night or the smoothness of the sheets?

Even though we go to sleep, Jesus is still awake. He even sends angels to watch over us. Jesus wants us to have a good night so we can have a good tomorrow. Sleep well tonight. Good night.

Dear Jesus,
    Thank You for nighttime and the chance to rest, and for keeping me safe when I sleep. Amen.

God was making all mankind His friends through Christ.
2 Corinthians 5:19

Real or Pretend?

Let's pretend to build a tower. Pretend to take one block at a time and put it on top. Count with me as you pretend to build the tower.

"One, two, three, four, five, six ... whoops! Be careful. Seven, eight ... It's getting taller ... nine, ten ... Can you keep going?"

What's going to happen to the tower soon? I heard a crash. What happened? That's okay, if the pretend tower fell. You can build another one later. You can imagine that you have blocks. Do you pretend to play other things, too?

One thing is real, and we don't have to pretend about it: Jesus loves us. Even though we can't see Jesus, He really cares about us. Jesus isn't pretend. He's real. We can imagine what He might look like. We can imagine how Jesus is dressed. But Jesus is real. He really loves us. Jesus is our Friend.

Dear Jesus
Thank You for being You. Amen.

A child lies quietly in its mother's arms.
Psalm 131:2–3

A True Story

One day Mommy was on the telephone. Jill and Mandy were goofing off. Jill jumped on the sofa and hit a table. She cried and cried. Her arm was broken, and it hurt a lot.

Jill's mommy took her to the hospital. Jill's daddy met them there. He held Jill. Jill kept crying.

Some people at the hospital took X-ray pictures of Jill's arm. A doctor put her arm in a cast. Then Jill went home. Jill's arm still hurt a lot. She started to feel better the next day.

On Sunday, Jill's mommy and daddy went to church. They prayed to God and thanked Him for helping Jill. What do you think Jill prayed about?

Dear Jesus,

Sometimes I get hurt. Sometimes accidents happen. Sometimes I just goof off. Please give me people to help take care of me. I know I can always talk to You about how I feel. Amen.

There was a wedding.
John 2:1–2

Happy Times

What an exciting day! There was going to be a wedding at church. People started arriving. Some were all dressed up. Everyone sat quietly. Then the organ started playing. A white cloth was pulled down the aisle. The wedding started.

Everything was lovely. There were lots of flowers. Everybody looked so happy! It was very exciting.

Now it was time for the reception. What a party! People danced and laughed and talked. Then it was time to go home.

Do you know someone who was in a wedding? Have you ever seen pictures of a wedding?

Dear Jesus,

Thank You for some exciting times. Even though I'm not very old, there are some things I will remember a long, long time. Thank You for the wonderful time I had when
_____. Amen.

God showed His love for us.
1 John 4:9

A Frosty Picture

Mario could hardly see through the window. Frost covered the glass. He started to draw a picture with his finger. Christmas was coming soon, so he drew a Christmas scene.

Take your finger and draw a Christmas picture in the air. Let's start with the stable. Now we need some people. Are you going to add animals? Keep working until your picture is done.

Mario's finger is getting wet and cold. Now he's done. Are you almost finished?

Oh, no! Mario's picture is starting to drip with water. There goes a cow. Now he can't see the manger at all. But he will still remember what is important about Christmas. Even without his frosty picture, Mario knows that Jesus was born at Christmas.

What is the most important thing for you about Christmas?

Prayer suggestion: Thank Jesus for the most important thing about Christmas.

Tell others that the Father sent His Son.
1 John 4:14

Happy Birthday, Dear Jesus

Christmas was coming! Today Brian was helping his mom get ready for a "Jesus birthday party." She was making the cake.

First Brian's mom made the batter. After the cake was baked and had cooled, Brian picked out his favorite frosting. What kind of frosting would you choose?

Then Brian put on the candles. How many candles would you put on a "Jesus birthday cake"?

Brian put 13 on the cake. That's because he found 13 candles in the box.

Soon his friends would come to celebrate Jesus' birthday. Brian had invited some children who didn't know much about Jesus. He wanted to tell them all about Christmas. Whom could you invite to a "Jesus birthday party"?

Dear Jesus,
I know all about Christmas. I know You were born in a manger. I know that shepherds and Wise Men visited You. Not everybody knows about Your birthday. Help me think of people I could tell about You. And happy birthday, dear Jesus! Amen.

245

God has been gracious to you.
Luke 1:30–33

How Do You Open Up Christmas?

Michael woke up slowly. The December air was cool, even underneath the covers. Suddenly, Michael was ready to jump out of bed. He had remembered something. Today was the day to open Christmas!

"When can we open Christmas, Mommy?" he asked right away.

"Later, Michael, later," Mommy replied.

Later in the morning, Michael asked again, "Is it time to open Christmas?"

"Not yet," Mommy answered.

"Is it time to open Christmas *now*?" Michael asked again and again. Always the answer was the same: not yet.

Finally, it was time.

Mommy stood on a ladder to reach the box from the top of the hall closet. "Now, Michael, you may open Christmas," she said.

Quickly but carefully, Michael unwound the thick strings that tied the box. He pulled off layers of newspaper. Then slowly, ever so slowly, he took out the pieces. A shepherd was on top. Then, an empty manger. Next, an angel. Finally, the box was empty.

As Michael arranged the figures on the table, he smiled. "Now that we've opened Christmas, it will feel like Christmas."

How do you open Christmas at your house?

Dear Jesus,

Help me remember that Christmas is Your birthday. Amen.

God sent His own Son.
Galatians 4:4–5

An Empty Christmas?

Grace carried the tray carefully. The cookies looked so pretty! She and her dad had worked hard in the kitchen. They mixed the dough, then rolled it out. Grace used Christmas cookie cutters to make the fancy shapes. Now the cookies were baked, frosted, and decorated. She carried the tray slowly up her neighbor's steps.

"Why, Grace! How nice to see you," said Mrs. Fritz. "How special to have cookies for Christmas," she said, smiling.

Grace looked around the apartment. Things were just the same as always. There wasn't a Christmas tree. There were no decorations. No presents were stacked up. A small manger scene was the only thing different.

"Mrs. Fritz," said Grace, "your Christmas is empty. Where are your presents? Don't you have any decorations?"

"No, Grace," said Mrs. Fritz. "But see the manger? That's all I need for a good Christmas."

How do you feel hearing about Mrs. Fritz? Was she right about Christmas?

Dear Jesus,

Thank You for all the wonderful things that make Christmas fun. Thanks especially for being born. Amen.

She will have a son, and you will name Him Jesus.
Matthew 1:20–23

The Smell of Christmas

Can you smell Christmas coming? What is the smell of Christmas at your house? Take a good sniff.

What were the smells of the first Christmas? Pretend you are in the stable with Mary and Joseph. Can you smell the animals? the hay? the warmth?

The smells of our Christmas celebration are different from the smells of the first Christmas. But there's something that is still the same: Christmas is still Jesus' birthday.

Christmas will always be Jesus' birthday.

Dear Jesus,

We're getting ready to celebrate Your birthday at our house. We can almost smell Christmas coming. I'm so glad You were born at Christmas. Amen.

So let us not become tired of doing good.
Galatians 6:9–10

Sharing Can Be Tough

Whitney was sorting through her toys. She wasn't happy about it though. The church was collecting toys for children who wouldn't have a Christmas present. Everyone was to bring something they didn't use anymore.

Whitney liked everything. She couldn't give away the big dump truck because she used that in the sand. The big stack of puzzles would be fun to use on a gloomy day in winter. Her dolls needed to sleep with her, even if they couldn't all fit on the bed.

"Whitney, what did you find?" Dad called. "I'll help you wrap it up." What did Whitney say?

Dear Jesus,

Sometimes sharing is so hard. Sometimes I want to keep everything for myself, and I don't want to let somebody play with my toys. Then I don't even like to share _____. Please help me share better. Amen.

Martha was upset.
Luke 10:38–42

When Shoes Don't Fit

Amanda was very excited. She was going to the Christmas service at church. She wore her favorite outfit. Her hair looked so nice. Now she would put on her shiny shoes.

"Oh, Mommy," Amanda cried. "My shoes are too tight."

Amanda tried to squeeze her feet into the shoes. Then Mommy helped, too. It didn't work. The shoes really were too tight.

"You'll just have to wear your other pair, Amanda," said Mommy. "It's almost time to go."

"I can't wear those shoes," cried Amanda. "Everybody will laugh at my feet."

What do you think happened?

Dear Jesus,

Everything doesn't always work out right. Everything doesn't always fit together. I get so upset sometimes! Please help me remember what's really important: You love me. Amen.

The Spirit produces love, joy, peace, patience . ...
Galatians 5:22

A Don't Day or a Do Day?

It was two o'clock. "Ouch," said Brandon.

"Brandon, *don't* touch that holly decoration; it's sharp."

It was three o'clock. "Mommy," Brandon said, "the lights just went out on the Christmas tree."

"Brandon, *don't* play with the cord. *Don't* go near those electric wires."

It was four o'clock. Crash went the tin of Christmas cookies. Guess what room Brandon was in now.

"Brandon, *don't* get into those Christmas goodies. *Don't* go near the kitchen," said Daddy.

Don't, don't, don't. For Brandon it seemed like a *don't* day instead of a Christmastime day. Brandon could have remembered the *dos* about Christmas. Let's help Brandon.

Do show kindness, like the shepherds showed baby Jesus. Brandon, *do* make a Christmas picture to give to someone. *Do* show love, like Mary and Joseph showed to baby Jesus. Brandon, *do* nice things, like picking up the toys and offering to help.

What else could Brandon *do*?

Dear Jesus,

Help me *do* loving things for others. Amen.

You know the way that leads
to the place where I am . ...
John 14:1–4

Window Shopping

"I want this," said Melita as she walked through the aisles of toys.

"Buy me this," begged Melita as she passed the building blocks.

"Look at that neat airplane," said Melita. "Can't I have that?"

Sometimes walking through a toy store before Christmas isn't much fun. You can't get everything you want.

Jesus gives us something for Christmas that we can't find in a store. It's not hiding behind the dolls. It's not between the covers of the new books. His present is that someday we will live with Him in heaven.

Even if we had money to buy all the toys in a store, we couldn't buy Jesus' gift. That's because His gift is a present. There isn't any checkout counter. There isn't any wrapping. And Jesus' present doesn't cost a single penny. He gives us heaven, free.

Dear Jesus,

I love to look at all the toys in the stores. Things look so pretty all ready for Christmas. Help me remember that Your present is coming some other time. Please help me be patient. Amen.

You did not choose Me; I chose you.
John 15:16–17

Puddles

It had rained and rained and rained. The ground was soaking wet. You could almost hear the earth go slurp, slurp. Because there was a lot of rain, there were also a lot of puddles.

What do you think about puddles? Do you ever do anything with puddles?

Tara was going outside. She wore her boots and took an umbrella. It had stopped raining, but she took her new umbrella anyway.

When Tara got outside, she headed for the biggest puddle. Splash, splash, splash. Tromp, tromp, tromp. Smush, smush, smush. What do you think Tara was doing?

Pretty soon, Tara was so wet she went back to the house. What do you think happened next?

Dear Jesus,

Sometimes it's hard to make decisions. I know what I should do, but sometimes I don't. Help me think about my choices, and help me do what is right. Amen.

God ... made His light shine in our hearts.
2 Corinthians 4:6

Nothing to Do

Andrew walked around the house. He looked in the bedroom. He walked to the kitchen. Then Andrew walked upstairs.

"Daddy, there's nothing to do," he complained.

"Why, Andrew! What about the things you got for Christmas?" Daddy asked.

"I'm tired of those," Andrew answered. "And I need new batteries."

"Why don't you rearrange the manger?" Daddy suggested.

"No, Christmas is over, and I don't feel like it anyway," Andrew answered.

"Change the Christmas tree ornaments. You can move them around and make the tree look different," Daddy said.

"No, no, no! Christmas is over. I don't even feel like Christmas anymore," Andrew said.

Do you feel like Andrew today? What would you suggest for Andrew to do?

Dear Jesus,

I know Christmas Day is finished. Help me remember to keep thanking You for coming at Christmas. Amen.

Jesus grew.
Luke 2:52

Growing Up and Up

I used to be one,
> And I had such fun.
> Do something you could do as a one-year-old.

I used to be two;
> See what I could do.
> Do something you could do as a two-year-old.

I used to be three;
> Take a look at growing-up me!
> Do something you could do as a three-year-old.

You've grown a lot since you were a baby. Who are some of the people who helped you grow? Those people used to be little, too. Everybody starts out as a baby.

Even Jesus was a baby, then a one-year-old, then a two-year-old, and He was even as old as you are now!

Dear Jesus,
> I'm glad You know how it feels to grow up. Amen.

Jesus Christ is the same … .
Hebrews 13:8

Good-bye

"Good-bye," Chelsea said sadly to her grandma. "I wish you didn't have to go."

"Good-bye," Todd waved through the car window. Todd waved to his old house. He was moving away.

"Good-bye," Justin waved to his teacher. "See you next week."

Have you waved good-bye to someone today? Let's see how you wave good-bye.

We are all waving good-bye to something today: an old year. Tomorrow we start a new calendar. We can wave hello to a new year tomorrow.

Waving good-bye can be happy. Waving good-bye can be sad—or a little happy and a little sad.

If you waved to Jesus, it wouldn't be for hello or good-bye. Jesus is always with us.

Dear Jesus,
I don't have to say good-bye to You this year because You're always with me. I like that. Amen.

Topical Index

Scripture Index